To

Dearest Nana,

with all my love,

Jane xx

11th June 2001

THE TIMES

Prayers and Readings
for All Occasions

THE TIMES

Prayers and Readings
for All Occasions

Compiled and edited by
Owen Collins

Fount
An Imprint of HarperCollins*Publishers*

HarperCollins*Publishers*
77–85 Fulham Palace Road, London W6 8JB
www.**fire**and**water**.com

The Times/Sunday Times is a registered
trademark of Times Newspapers Limited

First published in Great Britain in 2001 by
HarperCollins*Publishers*

1 3 5 7 9 10 8 6 4 2

Compilation copyright © 2001 Owen Collins

Owen Collins asserts the moral right to be identified
as the compiler of this work

A catalogue record for this book is available
from the British Library

ISBN 0 00 710355 7

Set in Bembo

Printed and bound in Great Britain by
Creative Print and Design (Wales), Ebbw Vale

CONTENTS

❀ Introduction   IX

PART ONE: SHORT PRAYERS AND MEDITATIONS

❀ Arrow Prayers   3
❀ Love Notes from Lovers of the Lord   6
❀ Short Prayers   8
❀ A Week of Psalms   12
❀ Meditations   22

PART TWO: THE DEVOTIONAL LIFE

❀ Abiding   51
❀ Praise and Thanksgiving   54
❀ Prayer   58
❀ Bible Reading   66
❀ Contemplation and Meditation   71
❀ Christian Belief   73
❀ Seeking Forgiveness   75
❀ Conversion and Commitment   80
❀ Baptism   83
❀ Doubt   85
❀ Assurance   88
❀ Dedication   91
❀ Holy Communion   105
❀ Growth in Holiness   110

Temptations 113
Spiritual Dryness and Trials 117
Renewal 118
Worship 122
The Body of Christ 125
Daily Prayers 126

PART THREE: EVERYDAY LIFE

Nature 147
Ambition and Guidance 151
Birthdays, New Year and Times of Life 153
Marriage and Home Life 156
Sickness 157
Stress 159
Fear and Times of Change 161
Worry and Difficulties 166
Persecution and Opposition 169
Work 170
Serving God 172
Serving Others 175
Sadness, Despair and Depression 180
Bereavement and the Death of a Child 185
Growing Old and Contemplating Death 187
Facing Death 192
Last Words of People About to Die 199
Heaven 206

PART FOUR: CHRISTIAN FESTIVALS AND THE CHRISTIAN YEAR

Sundays 209
Harvest 210
Advent 211
Christmas 211
Epiphany 216
Lent 217

❈　Easter (1) The Death of Christ　　218
❈　Easter (2) The Resurrection of Christ　　235
❈　Ascension　　241
❈　Pentecost　　241
❈　Trinity　　243
❈　The Return of Christ　　244

❈　Index of Sources　　247
❈　Index of First Lines　　257

INTRODUCTION

It is probably true that Christians have written more about prayer than any other topic. We find it easy to agree with J.C. Ryle, the first Anglican bishop of Liverpool, that 'Truly we have learned a great lesson when we have learned that "saying prayers" is not praying!' Many preachers tell us: 'Don't treat prayer like a slot machine; prayer is more than just praying a prayer and expecting God to answer automatically'; and 'Don't take a shopping list of petitions to God and think that you have finished praying when you have completed presenting the list to the Almighty.' But how do we move on? How do we pray? Countless Christians are helped by Ignatius of Loyola. In the preface to his *Spiritual Exercises* he wrote: 'Spiritual Exercises are for conquering oneself and ordering one's life without being influenced by any ungodly ideas', and 'It will be of immense benefit to the receiver of the Exercises to enter into them with a heart and a will that are wide open towards his Creator and Lord. He should offer his entire will and freedom so that his divine majesty may make use of his person and possessions according to his own most holy will.'

Some people find it a great help to choose one short thought to carry with them throughout the day. The short meditations, arrow prayers, and 'Love notes from Lovers of the Lord' from Part One have been added for this purpose. In that section there is also a selection of psalms for meditation, one for each day of the week. The Book of Psalms consists of one hundred and fifty spiritual songs and was the hymn book of godly Jews. While they cover a wide range of topics, they especially concentrate on the themes of praise and prayer.

When John Wesley, in the middle of the eighteenth-century revival, wanted Methodists to gain the greatest benefit from hymn-singing he gave them practical instructions, but ended with straightforward spiritual advice:

Learn the tune.
Sing them as they are printed.
Sing all. 'If it is a cross to you, take it up and you will find a
*   blessing.'*
Sing lustily and with a good courage.
Sing modestly. Do not bawl.
Sing in time. Do not run before or stay behind.

Above all, sing spiritually. Have an eye to God in every word
you sing. Aim at pleasing Him more than yourself, or any other
creature. In order to do this, attend strictly to the sense of what
you sing, and see that your heart is not carried away with the
sound, but offered to God continually.

Thomas Fuller has pointed out that it is best to 'Pray *now*, for when changes, crisis, difficulties come: i.e. "Lord, teach me the art of patience while I am well, and enable me to use of it when I am sick. In that day either lighten my burden or strengthen my back. Make me, who so often in my health have discovered my weakness in presuming on my own strength, to be strong in my sickness when I solely rely on your assistance." ' To this end Part Two, 'The Devotional Life', gives a range of prayers and readings which are designed to build up our spiritual life.

The centrepiece of this book comes in Part Three, with a selection of prayers and readings for 'Everyday Life', ranging from giving thanks to God for nature and birthdays, to marriage and home life, to sickness, stress, fear, worry and opposition, to work, serving God and serving other people, to sadness, bereavement, and to, finally, facing death and heaven. The 'last words' of forty-one famous Christians on their death-beds are included here. The more we are in tune with God, the more valuable these prayers become to us.

Part Four consists of a shorter section of prayers and readings focusing on the Christian year, from Advent through to the Return of Christ.

What has been termed 'devotional' reading appears to be on the wane among Christians who lead such frenetically busy lives in the twenty-first century. 'Seek in reading and you will find in meditation; knock in prayer and it will be opened to you in contemplation,' advised John of the Cross. 'In all things I sought quiet, and found it not save in retirement and in books,' testified Thomas à Kempis. The American philosopher, theologian and revival preacher Jonathan Edwards affirmed that 'Christian devotional reading helps us find intimate union with God, its motivation being to love God with all our heart, mind, and will.'

Wise Christians from previous generations have pointed out that it is not the amount of reading that is important but how one reads that matters. In Part One there are thirty-one 'articles' from Archbishop François Fénelon's *Maxims of the saints*, which provide a month's material for meditation and for daily devotional reading. In one of his letters Fénelon told a Christian lady, 'It is preferable to be very humble and ashamed of the faults one has committed than to be satisfied with one's meditation and puffed up with the idea that one is very advanced in spiritual matters.' In another letter, to the Duchesse de Beauvilliers, Fénelon gave this advice about meditation: 'When you meditate, imagine that Jesus Christ in person is about to talk to you about the most important thing in the world. Give him your complete attention.'

OWEN COLLINS

PART ONE

SHORT PRAYERS
AND MEDITATIONS

Arrow Prayers

E.B. Pusey

Have some arrow prayers to pray during the day, or a psalm.

And by his stripes we are healed.

And I know He loveth me!

And they shall be my people.

And to him my soul shall live.

And we shall be his people.

Arise! Shine! Thy light has come!

Awake, O my soul, awake!

Be gracious to me, O God.

Because of me you bear fruit.

Beside the waters of peace.

But God is rich in mercy.

Come, thou Father of the poor.

Create a clean heart in me.

Fill me with joy and gladness.

For God is at work in me.

For there is no other name.

Glory to the Lamb of God.

Go and bear fruit that will last.

God is worthy of our praise.

Grace and glory he bestows.

Have mercy on me, O God.

He let us share in His spirit.

Him alone you shall adore.

His eye is on the sparrow.

His love is everlasting.

His praise endures forever.

Holy, holy, holy Lord.

Holy is the Lamb of God.

How good is the Lord to all.

How right it is to love you.

I have been given mercy.

I have called you by your name.

I have grasped you by the hand.

I sought Him whom my heart loves.

I will never forget you.

In his quiver he hid me.

In you I hope all day long.

In you I place all my trust.

In your love remember me.

Jesus is the Lamb of God.

Joy cometh in the morning.

Keep us steadfast in your love.

Keep your eyes fixed on Jesus.

Let go and let God.

Let silence be your wisdom.

Let the healing waters flow.

My cup is overflowing.

My God, make haste to help me!

My grace is enough for you.

My Heavenly Father knows.

My life is spent with sorrow.

My peace is my gift to you.

My soul magnifies the Lord.

O come, let us adore Him.

O my strength, for you I watch.

O, that we might know the Lord!

Only in God be at rest.

Remember your mercies, Lord.

Seek the things that are above.

Taste and see that the Lord is good.

The Father and I are one.

The hand of the Lord feeds me.

The Lord keeps the little ones.

The love of Christ compels us.

The victory of justice.

Think upon all His wonders.

We have been given mercy.

Who is this king of glory?

With God I shall do bravely.

Worth more than many sparrows.

Worthy is the Lamb of God.

You are my strength and my song.

You have been given mercy.

Love Notes from Lovers of the Lord

St Margaret of Scotland

Take for your motto: Love has conquered me, it alone shall possess my heart.

Julian of Norwich

He is our clothing. In His love He wraps and holds us. He enfolds us for love and He will never let us go.

Teresa of Avila *1515 – 82. Spanish Carmelite Mystic.*

Love does not consist in shedding tears, nor in tasting sweetness and that tenderness in which one seeks consolation; it consists in serving God in justice, in strength of soul, and in humility.

Catherine of Siena

Eternal goodness, You want me to gaze into You and see that You love me, to see that You love me gratuitously, so that I may love everyone with the very same love.

C.S. Lewis

I am in Love, and out of it I will not go.

Augustine

Let the root of love be within. Of this root nothing can spring but what is good.

Thérèse of Lisieux

I do not regret that I have given myself to love.

Remember that nothing is small in the eyes of God. Do all that you do with love.

Francis de Sales

So we must either love or die, because he who does not love remains a dead person.

Thomas à Kempis

A wise lover values not so much the gift of the lover, as the love of the giver. He esteems the affection above the gift, and values every gift far below the Beloved. A noble lover is not content with a gift, but desires Myself above all gifts.

Love is a mighty power, a great and complete good; Love alone lightens every burden, and makes the rough places smooth. It bears every hardship as though it were nothing, and renders all bitterness sweet and acceptable. The love of Jesus is noble, and inspires us to great deeds; it moves us always to desire perfection.

Let my soul spend itself in Your praise, rejoicing for love.

Pope John XXIII

He who has a heart full of love always has something to give.

Thomas Aquinas

To love God is something greater than to know him.

Bernard of Clairvaux

We should love God because He is God, and the measure of our love should be to love Him without measure.

Francis de Sales

All that you do for love is love. Fatigue and even death itself accepted for motives of love is nothing else but love! How happy are those who love the cross and carry it generously. It will appear in all its glory in the heavens when Christ our Lord will come to judge the living and the dead. Heaven is the altar for all who are crucified; therefore, let us love the crosses that we meet as we go through life.

Author unknown

O Heart of Love, I believe in Your goodness, I hope in Your mercy, I trust in Your love.

Jean-Pierre de Caussade

Let us love, for love will give us everything.

J.H. Newman

Complete Thy work, O Lord, and as Thou hast loved me from the beginning, so make me to love Thee unto the end.

Short Prayers

Psalm 70:1 NRSV

Be pleased, O God, to deliver me.
 O LORD, make haste to help me!

Psalm 103:1 NRSV

Bless the LORD, O my soul,
 and all that is within me,
 bless his holy name.

A Chinese student

Change the world, O Lord, beginning with me.

Revelation 22:20 AV

Come, Lord Jesus.

John Chrysostom
Glory to God for all things.

Praying tax-collector, Luke 18:13 AV
God be merciful to me, a sinner.

2 Timothy 4:22 AV
Grace be with you.

William Barclay
Help me, O God, like Jesus to be growing all the time.

Mary, Luke 1:38 NRSV
Here am I, the servant of the Lord; let it be with me according to your word.

Father of boy possessed by an unclean spirit, Mark 9:24 AV
Lord, I believe; help thou mine unbelief.

J.H. Newman
I ask not to see; I ask not to know; I ask only to be used.

John Wesley
Jesus, strengthen my desire to work and speak and think for you.

Penitent dying thief, Luke 23:42 AV
Lord, remember me when thou comest into thy kingdom.

John Calvin
Let our chief goal, O God, be your glory, and to enjoy you for ever.

Psalm 19:14 NRSV
*Let the words of my mouth and the meditation of my heart
  be acceptable to you,
    O LORD, my rock and my redeemer.*

Lancelot Andrewes

Let this day, O Lord, add some knowledge or good deed to yesterday.

The Jesus Prayer

The Eastern Orthodox Church teaches that this prayer is to be said many times regularly during the day.

Lord Jesus Christ, Son of God, have mercy on me, a sinner.

Abraham Lincoln

Lord, give us faith that right makes might.

Michelangelo

Lord, make me see your glory in every place.

Augustine

Lord, give me what you are requiring of me.

Brother Lawrence

Lord, make me according to your heart.

King Charles I

Lord, let your glory be my goal, your word my rule, and then your will be done.

Peter, Matthew 14:30 AV

Lord, save me.

A Canaanite woman, Matthew 15:25 AV

Lord, help me.

The Meditation Prayer of Francis of Assisi

My God and My All!

Thomas, John 20:28 AV

My Lord and my God.

William Penn

O God, help us not to despise or oppose what we do not understand.

John Donne

O Lord, never allow us to think we can stand by ourselves and not need you, our greatest need.

John Wesley

O Lord, let us not live to be useless, for Christ's sake.

Psalm 43:3 NRSV

O send out your light and your truth;
  let them lead me;
let them bring me to your holy hill
  and to your dwelling.

Psalm 69:5 NRSV

O God, you know my folly;
  the wrongs I have done are not hidden from you.

Gladys Aylward

O God, give me strength.

William Barclay

O God, keep me from being difficult to live with.

W.M. Thackeray

Pray God, keep us simple.

Samuel, I Samuel 3:10 NRSV

Speak, for your servant is listening.

François Fénelon

Teach me to pray. Pray yourself in me.

Jeremy Taylor

Teach us to pray often, that we may pray oftener.

Thomas More

The things, good Lord, that we pray for, give us the grace to labour for.

Revelation 22:20 NRSV

The grace of the Lord Jesus be with all the saints. Amen.

Psalm 27:14 NRSV

Wait for the LORD;
*   be strong, and let your heart take courage;*
*   wait for the LORD!*

Psalm 85:6 NRSV

Will you not revive us again,
*   so that your people may rejoice in you?*

Augustine

You have made us for yourself and our hearts are restless until in you they find their rest.

A Week of Psalms
Sunday: Worship

Psalm 84 NRSV

How lovely is your dwelling place,
*   O LORD of hosts!*
My soul longs, indeed it faints
*   for the courts of the LORD;*
my heart and my flesh sing for joy
*   to the living God.*

Even the sparrow finds a home,
*   and the swallow a nest for herself,*
*   where she may lay her young,*
at your altars, O LORD of hosts,
*   my King and my God.*

Happy are those who live in your house,
  ever singing your praise. (Selah)

Happy are those whose strength is in you,
  in whose heart are the highways to Zion.
As they go through the valley of Baca
  they make it a place of springs;
  the early rain also covers it with pools.
They go from strength to strength;
  the God of gods will be seen in Zion.

O LORD God of hosts, hear my prayer;
  give ear, O God of Jacob! (Selah)
Behold our shield, O God;
  look on the face of your anointed.

For a day in your courts is better
  than a thousand elsewhere.
I would rather be a doorkeeper in the house of my God
  than live in the tents of wickedness.
For the LORD God is a sun and shield;
  he bestows favour and honour.
No good thing does the LORD withhold
  from those who walk uprightly.
O LORD of hosts,
  happy is everyone who trusts in you.

Monday: Forgiven

Psalm 32 NRSV
Happy are those whose transgression is forgiven,
  whose sin is covered.
Happy are those to whom the LORD imputes no iniquity,
and in whose spirit there is no deceit.

While I kept silence, my body wasted away
  through my groaning all day long.
For day and night your hand was heavy upon me;
my strength was dried up as by the heat of summer. (Selah)

Then I acknowledged my sin to you,
  and I did not hide my iniquity;
I said, 'I will confess my transgressions to the LORD,'
  and you forgave the guilt of my sin. (Selah)

Therefore let all who are faithful
  offer prayer to you;
at a time of distress, the rush of mighty waters
  shall not reach them.
You are a hiding place for me;
  you preserve me from trouble;
  you surround me with glad cries of deliverance. (Selah)

I will instruct you and teach you the way you should go;
  I will counsel you with my eye upon you.
Do not be like a horse or a mule, without understanding,
  whose temper must be curbed with bit and bridle,
  else it will not stay near you.

Many are the torments of the wicked,
  but steadfast love surrounds those who trust in the LORD.
Be glad in the LORD and rejoice, O righteous,
  and shout for joy, all you upright in heart.

Tuesday: Consecration

Psalm 116 NRSV
I love the LORD, because he has heard
  my voice and my supplications.
Because he inclined his ear to me,
  therefore I will call on him as long as I live.

The snares of death encompassed me;
  the pangs of Sheol laid hold on me;
  I suffered distress and anguish.
Then I called on the name of the LORD:
  'O LORD, *I pray, save my life!'*

Gracious is the LORD, *and righteous;*
  our God is merciful.
The LORD *protects the simple;*
  when I was brought low, he saved me.
Return, O my soul, to your rest,
  for the LORD *has dealt bountifully with you.*

For you have delivered my soul from death,
  my eyes from tears,
  my feet from stumbling.
I walk before the LORD
  in the land of the living.
I kept my faith, even when I said,
  'I am greatly afflicted';
I said in my consternation,
  'Everyone is a liar.'

What shall I return to the LORD
  for all his bounty to me?
I will lift up the cup of salvation
  and call on the name of the LORD,
I will pay my vows to the LORD
  in the presence of all his people.
Precious in the sight of the LORD
  is the death of his faithful ones.
O LORD, *I am your servant;*
  I am your servant, the child of your serving girl.
  You have loosed my bonds.
I will offer to you a thanksgiving sacrifice
  and call on the name of the LORD.
I will pay my vows to the LORD

in the presence of all his people,
in the courts of the house of the LORD,
    in your midst, O Jerusalem.
Praise the LORD!

Wednesday: God's care

Psalm 121 NRSV
I lift up my eyes to the hills –
    from where will my help come?
My help comes from the LORD,
    who made heaven and earth.

He will not let your foot be moved;
    he who keeps you will not slumber.
He who keeps Israel
    will neither slumber nor sleep.

The LORD is your keeper;
    the LORD is your shade at your right hand.
The sun shall not strike you by day,
    nor the moon by night.

The LORD will keep you from all evil;
    he will keep your life.
The LORD will keep
    your going out and your coming in
    from this time on and for evermore.

Thursday: Taught by God

Psalm 25 NRSV
To you, O LORD, I lift up my soul.
O my God, in you I trust;
    do not let me be put to shame;

do not let my enemies exult over me.
Do not let those who wait for you be put to shame;
  let them be ashamed who are wantonly treacherous.

Make me to know your ways, O LORD;
  teach me your paths.
Lead me in your truth, and teach me,
  for you are the God of my salvation;
  for you I wait all day long.

Be mindful of your mercy, O LORD, and of your steadfast love,
  for they have been from of old.
Do not remember the sins of my youth or my transgressions;
  according to your steadfast love remember me,
  for your goodness' sake, O LORD!

Good and upright is the LORD;
  therefore he instructs sinners in the way.
He leads the humble in what is right,
  and teaches the humble his way.
All the paths of the Lord are steadfast love and faithfulness,
for those who keep his covenant and his decrees.

For your name's sake, O LORD,
  pardon my guilt, for it is great.
Who are they that fear the LORD?
  He will teach them the way that they should choose.
They will abide in prosperity,
  and their children shall possess the land.
The friendship of the LORD is for those who fear him,
  and he makes his covenant known to them.
My eyes are ever toward the LORD,
  for he will pluck my feet out of the net.

Turn to me and be gracious to me,
  for I am lonely and afflicted.
Relieve the troubles of my heart,

and bring me out of my distress.
Consider my affliction and my trouble,
  and forgive all my sins.

Consider how many are my foes,
  and with what violent hatred they hate me.
O guard my life, and deliver me;
  do not let me be put to shame, for I take refuge in you.
May integrity and uprightness preserve me,
  for I wait for you.

Redeem Israel, O God,
  out of all its troubles.

Friday: Affliction

Psalm 69 NRSV
Save me, O God,
  for the waters have come up to my neck.
I sink in deep mire,
  where there is no foothold;
I have come into deep waters,
  and the flood sweeps over me.
I am weary with my crying;
  my throat is parched.
My eyes grow dim
  with waiting for my God.

More in number than the hairs of my head
  are those who hate me without cause;
many are those who would destroy me,
  my enemies who accuse me falsely.
What I did not steal
  must I now restore?
O God, you know my folly;
  the wrongs I have done are not hidden from you.

Do not let those who hope in you be put to shame because of me,
 O LORD God of hosts;
do not let those who seek you be dishonoured because of me,
 O God of Israel.
It is for your sake that I have borne reproach,
 that shame has covered my face.
I have become a stranger to my kindred,
 an alien to my mother's children.

It is zeal for your house that has consumed me;
 the insults of those who insult you have fallen on me.
When I humbled my soul with fasting,
 they insulted me for doing so.
When I made sackcloth my clothing,
 I became a byword to them.
I am the subject of gossip for those who sit in the gate,
 and the drunkards make songs about me.

But as for me, my prayer is to you, O LORD.
 At an acceptable time, O God,
 in the abundance of your steadfast love, answer me.
With your faithful help rescue me
 from sinking in the mire;
let me be delivered from my enemies
 and from the deep waters.
Do not let the flood sweep over me,
 or the deep swallow me up,
 or the Pit close its mouth over me.

Answer me, O LORD, for your steadfast love is good;
 according to your abundant mercy, turn to me.
Do not hide your face from your servant,
 for I am in distress — make haste to answer me.
Draw near to me, redeem me,
 set me free because of my enemies.

You know the insults I receive,
    and my shame and dishonour;
    my foes are all known to you.
Insults have broken my heart,
    so that I am in despair.
I looked for pity, but there was none;
    and for comforters, but I found none.
They gave me poison for food,
    and for my thirst they gave me vinegar to drink.

Let their table be a trap for them,
    a snare for their allies.
Let their eyes be darkened so that they cannot see,
    and make their loins tremble continually.
Pour out your indignation upon them,
    and let your burning anger overtake them.
May their camp be a desolation;
    let no one live in their tents.
For they persecute those whom you have struck down,
    and those whom you have wounded, they attack still more.
Add guilt to their guilt;
    may they have no acquittal from you.
Let them be blotted out of the book of the living;
    let them not be enrolled among the righteous.
But I am lowly and in pain;
    let your salvation, O God, protect me.

I will praise the name of God with a song;
    I will magnify him with thanksgiving.
This will please the LORD more than an ox
    or a bull with horns and hoofs.
Let the oppressed see it and be glad;
    you who seek God, let your hearts revive.
For the Lord hears the needy,
    and does not despise his own that are in bonds.

Let heaven and earth praise him,
 the seas and everything that moves in them.
For God will save Zion
 and rebuild the cities of Judah;
and his servants shall live there and possess it;
 the children of his servants shall inherit it,
 and those who love his name shall live in it.

Saturday: Praise

Psalm 103 NRSV

Bless the LORD, O my soul,
 and all that is within me,
 bless his holy name.
Bless the LORD, O my soul,
 and do not forget all his benefits —
who forgives all your iniquity,
 who heals all your diseases,
who redeems your life from the Pit,
 who crowns you with steadfast love and mercy,
who satisfies you with good as long as you live
 so that your youth is renewed like the eagle's.
The LORD works vindication
 and justice for all who are oppressed.
He made known his ways to Moses,
 his acts to the people of Israel.
The LORD is merciful and gracious,
 slow to anger and abounding in steadfast love.
He will not always accuse,
 nor will he keep his anger for ever.
He does not deal with us according to our sins,
 nor repay us according to our iniquities.
For as the heavens are high above the earth,
 so great is his steadfast love toward those who fear him;
as far as the east is from the west,
 so far he removes our transgressions from us.

As a father has compassion for his children,
so the LORD has compassion for those who fear him.
For he knows how we were made;
he remembers that we are dust.

As for mortals, their days are like grass;
they flourish like a flower of the field;
for the wind passes over it, and it is gone,
and its place knows it no more.
But the steadfast love of the LORD is from everlasting to everlasting
on those who fear him,
and his righteousness to children's children,
to those who keep his covenant
and remember to do his commandments.

The LORD has established his throne in the heavens,
and his kingdom rules over all.
Bless the LORD, O you his angels,
you mighty ones who do his bidding,
obedient to his spoken word.
Bless the LORD, all his hosts,
his ministers that do his will.
Bless the LORD, all his works,
in all places of his dominion.
Bless the LORD, O my soul.

Meditations
Our Father

Matthew 6:9–13 NRSV
Our Father in heaven,
hallowed be your name.
Your kingdom come.
Your will be done,
on earth as it is in heaven.
Give us this day our daily bread.

And forgive us our debts,
　　as we also have forgiven our debtors.
And do not bring us to the time of trial,
　　but rescue us from the evil one.

By your will they existed

Revelation 4:11; 7:12; 15:3–4 NRSV
You are worthy, our Lord and God,
　　to receive glory and honour and power,
for you created all things,
　　and by your will they existed and were created...

Amen! Blessing and glory and wisdom
and thanksgiving and honour
and power and might
be to our God for ever and ever!
　　Amen...

Great and amazing are your deeds,
　　Lord God the Almighty!
Just and true are your ways,
　　King of the nations!
Lord, who will not fear
　　and glorify your name?
For you alone are holy.
　　All nations will come
　　and worship before you,
for your judgements have been revealed.

Maxims of the saints

François Fénelon, taken from Thomas Cogswell Upham, **Life and Religious Opinions and Experience of Madame de la Mothe Guyon, 1847.**

Article one

Of the love of God, there are various kinds. At least, there are various feelings which go under that name.

First, there is what may be called mercenary or selfish love; that is, that love of God which originates in a sole regard to our own happiness. Those who love God with no other love than this, love Him just as the miser his money, and the voluptuous man his pleasures; attaching no value to God, except as a means to an end; and that end is the gratification of themselves. Such love, if it can be called by that name, is unworthy of God. He does not ask it; He will not receive it. In the language of Francis de Sales, 'it is sacrilegious and impious'.

Second, another kind of love does not exclude a regard to our own happiness as a motive of love, but requires this motive to be subordinate to a much higher one, namely, that of a regard to God's glory. It is a mixed state, in which we regard ourselves and God at the same time. This love is not necessarily selfish and wrong. On the contrary, when the two objects of it, God and ourselves, are relatively in the right position, that is to say, when we love God as He ought to be loved, and love ourselves no more than we ought to be loved, it is a love which, in being properly subordinated, is unselfish and is right.

Article two

1 Of the subjects of this mixed love all are not equally advanced.
2 Mixed love becomes pure love, when the love of self is relatively, though not absolutely, lost in a regard to the will of God. This is always the case, when the two objects are loved in their due proportion. So that pure love is mixed love when it is combined rightly.

3 Pure love is not inconsistent with mixed love, but is mixed love carried to its true result. When this result is attained, the motive of God's glory so expands itself, and so fills the mind, that the other motive, that of our own happiness, becomes so small, and so recedes from our inward notice, as to be practically annihilated. It is then that God becomes what He ever ought to be – the centre of the soul, to which all its affections tend; the great moral sun of the soul, from which all its light and all its warmth proceed. It is then that a man thinks no more of himself. He has become the man of a 'single eye'. His own happiness, and all that regards himself, is entirely lost sight of in his simple and fixed look to God's will and God's glory.

4 We lay ourselves at His feet. Self is known no more; not because it is wrong to regard and to desire our own good, but because the object of desire is withdrawn from our notice. When the sun shines, the stars disappear. When God is in the soul who can think of himself? So that we love God, and God alone; and all other things in and for God.

Article three

In the early periods of religious experience, motives, which have a regard to our personal happiness, are more prominent and effective than at later periods; nor are they to be condemned. It is proper, in addressing even religious men, to appeal to the fear of death, to the impending judgements of God, to the terrors of hell and the joys of heaven. Such appeals are recognized in the Holy Scriptures, and are in accordance with the views and feelings of good men in all ages of the world. The motives involved in them are powerful aids to beginners in religion; assisting, as they do, very much in repressing the passions, and in strengthening the practical virtues.

We should not think lightly, therefore, of the grace of God, as manifested in that inferior form of religion which stops short of the more glorious and perfected form of pure love. We are to follow God's grace, and not to go before it. To the higher state of pure love we are to advance step by step; watching carefully God's inward and outward providence; and receiving increased grace by improving the grace we have, till the dawning light becomes the perfect day.

Article four

He who is in the state of pure or perfect love, has all the moral and Christian virtues in himself. If temperance, forbearance, chastity, truth, kindness, forgiveness, justice, may be regarded as virtues, there can be no doubt that they are all included in holy love. That is to say, the principle of love will not fail to develop itself in each of these forms. St Augustine remarks that love is the foundation, source, or principle of all the virtues. This view is sustained also by St Francis de Sales and by Thomas Aquinas.

The state of pure love does not exclude the mental state which is called Christian hope. Hope in the Christian, when we analyse it into its elements, may be described as the desire of being united with God in heaven, accompanied with the expectation or belief of being so.

Article five

Souls that, by being perfected in love, are truly the subjects of sanctification, do not cease, nevertheless, to grow in grace. It may not be easy to specify and describe the degrees of sanctification; but there seem to be at least two modifications of experience after persons have reached this state.

1 The first may be described as the state of holy resignation. Such a soul thinks more frequently than it will, at a subsequent period, of its own happiness.
2 The second state is that of holy indifference. Such a soul absolutely ceases either to desire or to will, except in co-operation with the Divine leading. Its desires for itself, as it has greater light, are more completely and permanently merged in the one higher and more absorbing desire of God's glory, and the fulfilment of His will. In this state of experience, ceasing to do what we shall be likely to do, and what we may very properly do in a lower state, we no longer desire our own salvation merely as an eternal deliverance, or merely as involving the

greatest amount of personal happiness; but we desire it chiefly as the fulfilment of God's pleasure, and as resulting in His glory, and because He Himself desires and wills that we should thus desire and will.

3 Holy indifference is not inactivity. It is the furthest possible from it. It is indifference to anything and everything out of God's will; but it is the highest life and activity to anything and everything in that will.

Article six

One of the clearest and best established maxims of holiness is that the holy soul, when arrived at the second state mentioned, ceases to have desires for anything out of the will of God. The holy soul, when it is really in the state called the state of non-desire, may, nevertheless, desire everything in relation to the correction of its imperfections and weaknesses, its perseverance in its religious state, and its ultimate salvation, which it has reason to know from the Scriptures, or in any other way, that God desires. It may also desire all temporal good, houses and lands, food and clothing, friends and books, and exemption from physical suffering, and anything else, so far and only so far, as it has reason to think that such desire is coincident with the Divine desire. The holy soul not only desires particular things, sanctioned by the known will of God; but also the fulfilment of His will in all respects, unknown as well as known. Being in faith, it commits itself to God in darkness as well as in light. Its non-desire is simply its not desiring anything out of God

Article seven

In the history of inward experience, we not infrequently find accounts of individuals whose inward life may properly be characterized as extraordinary. They represent themselves as having extraordinary communications: dreams, visions, revelations. Without stopping to inquire whether these inward results arise from an excited and disordered state of the physical system or from God, the important remark to be made here is that these things, to whatever extent they may exist, do not constitute holiness.

The principle, which is the life of common Christians in their common mixed state, is the principle which originates and sustains the life of those who are truly 'the pure in heart', namely, the principle of faith working by love – existing, however, in the case of those last mentioned, in a greatly increased degree. This is obviously the doctrine of John of the Cross, who teaches us that we must walk in the night of faith; that is to say, with night around us, which exists in consequence of our entire ignorance of what is before us, and with faith alone, faith in God, in His Word, and in his Providences, for the soul's guide.

Again, the persons who have, or are supposed to have, the visions and other remarkable states to which we have referred are sometimes disposed to make their own experience, imperfect as it obviously is, the guide of their life, considered as separate from and as above the written law. Great care should be taken against such an error as this. God's word is our true rule.

Nevertheless, there is no interpreter of the Divine Word like that of a holy heart; or, what is the same thing, of the Holy Ghost dwelling in the heart. If we give ourselves wholly to God, the Comforter will take up His abode with us, and guide us into all that truth which will be necessary for us. Truly holy souls, therefore, continually looking to God for a proper understanding of His Word, may confidently trust that He will guide them aright. A holy soul, in the exercise of its legitimate powers of interpretation, may deduce important views from the Word of God which would not otherwise be known; but it cannot add anything to it.

Again, God is the regulator of the affections, as well as of the outward actions. Sometimes the state which He inspires within us is that of holy love; sometimes He inspires affections which have love and faith for their basis, but have a specific character, and then appear under other names, such as humility, forgiveness, gratitude. But in all cases there is nothing holy, except what is based upon the antecedent or 'prevenient' grace of God. In all the universe, there is but one legitimate Originator. Man's business is that of concurrence. And this view is applicable to all the stages of Christian experience, from the lowest to the highest.

Article eight

Writers often speak of abandonment. The term has a meaning somewhat specific. The soul in this state does not renounce everything, and thus become brutish in its indifference; but renounces everything except God's will.

Souls in the state of abandonment, not only forsake outward things, but, what is still more important, forsake themselves.

Abandonment, or self-renunciation, is not the renunciation of faith or of love or of anything else, except selfishness.

The state of abandonment, or entire self-renunciation, is generally attended, and perhaps we may say, carried out and perfected, by temptations more or less severe. We cannot well know, whether we have renounced ourselves, except by being tried on those very points to which our self-renunciation, either real or supposed, relates. One of the severest inward trials is that by which we are taken off from all inward sensible supports, and are made to live and walk by faith alone. Pious and holy men who have been the subjects of inward crucifixion, often refer to the trials which have been experienced by them. They sometimes speak of them as a sort of inward and terrible purgatory. 'Only mad and wicked men,' says Cardinal Bona, 'will deny the existence of these remarkable experiences, attested as they are by men of the most venerable virtue, who speak only of what they have known in themselves.'

Trials are not always of the same duration. The more cheerfully and faithfully we give ourselves to God, to be smitten in any and all of our idols, whenever and wherever He chooses, the shorter will be the work. God makes us to suffer no longer than He sees to be necessary for us.

We should not be premature in concluding that inward crucifixion is complete, and our abandonment to God is without any reservation whatever. The act of consecration, which is a sort of incipient step, may be sincere; but the reality of the consecration can be known only when God has applied the appropriate tests. The trial will show whether we are wholly the Lord's. Those who prematurely draw the conclusion that they are so, expose themselves to great illusion and injury.

Article nine

The state of abandonment, or of entire self-renunciation, does not take from the soul that moral power which is essential to its moral agency; nor that antecedent or prevenient grace, without which even abandonment itself would be a state of moral death; nor the principle of faith, which prevenient grace originated, and through which it now operates; nor the desire and hope of final salvation, although it takes away all uneasiness and unbelief connected with such a desire; nor the fountains of love which spring up deeply and freshly within it; nor the hatred of sin; nor the testimony of a good conscience.

But it takes away that uneasy hankering of the soul after pleasure either inward or outward, and the selfish vivacity and eagerness of nature, which is too impatient to wait calmly and submissively for God's time of action. By fixing the mind wholly upon God, it takes away the disposition of the soul to occupy itself with reflex acts; that is, with the undue examination and analysis of its own feelings. It does not take away the pain and sorrow naturally incident to our physical state and natural sensibilities; but it takes away all uneasiness, all murmuring; leaving the soul in its inner nature, and in every part of its nature where the power of faith reaches, calm and peaceable as the God that dwells there.

Article ten

God has promised life and happiness to His people. What He has promised can never fail to take place. Nevertheless, it is the disposition of those who love God with a perfect heart, to leave themselves entirely in His hands, irrespective, in some degree, of the promise. By the aid of the promise, without which they must have remained in their original weakness, they rise, as it were, above the promise; and rest in that essential and eternal will, in which the promise originated.

So much is this the case, that some individuals, across whose path God had spread the darkness of His providences, and who seemed to themselves for a time to be thrown out of His favour and to be hopelessly lost, have acquiesced with submission in the terrible destiny which was thus presented before them. Such was the state of mind of Francis de Sales, as he prostrated himself in the church of St Stephen des Grez. The language of such people, uttered without complaint, is, 'My God, my God, why hast thou forsaken me?' They claim God as their God, and will not abandon their love to Him, although they believe, at the time, that they are forsaken of Him. They choose to leave themselves, under all possible circumstances, entirely in the hands of God: their language is, even if it should be His pleasure to separate them for ever from the enjoyments of His presence, 'Not my will, but thine be done.'

It is perhaps difficult to perceive, how minds whose life, as it were, is the principle of faith, can be in this situation. Take the case of the Saviour. It is certainly difficult to conceive how the Saviour, whose faith never failed, could yet believe Himself forsaken; and yet it was so.

We know that it is impossible for God to forsake those who put their trust in Him. He can just as soon forsake His own word; and, what is more, He can just as soon forsake His own nature. Holy souls, nevertheless, may sometimes, in a way and under circumstances which we may not fully understand, believe themselves to be forsaken, beyond all possibility of hope; and yet such is their faith in God and their love to Him, that the will of God, even under such circumstances, is dearer to them than anything and everything else.

Article eleven
Those in the highest state of religious experience desire nothing, except that God may be glorified in them by the accomplishment of His holy will. Nor is it inconsistent with this, that holy souls possess that natural love which exists in the form of love for themselves. Their natural love, however, which, within its proper degree, is innocent love, is so absorbed in the love of God, that it ceases, for the most part, to be a distinct object of consciousness; and practically and truly they may be said to love themselves *in* and *for* God. Adam, in his state of innocence, loved himself, considered as the reflex image of God and for God's sake. So that we

may either say, that he loved God in himself, or that he loved himself *in* and *for* God. And it is because holy souls, extending their affections beyond their own limit, love their neighbour on the same principle of loving, namely, *in* and *for* God, that they may be said to love their neighbours as themselves.

It does not follow, because the love of ourselves is lost in the love of God, that we are to take no care, and to exercise no watch over ourselves. No man will be so seriously and constantly watchful over himself as he who loves himself in and for God alone. Having the image of God in himself, he has a motive strong, we might perhaps say, as that which controls the actions of angels, to guard and protect it.

It may be thought, perhaps, that this is inconsistent with the principle in the doctrines of holy living, which requires in the highest stages of inward experience, to avoid those reflex acts which consist in self-inspection, because such acts have a tendency to turn the mind off from God. The apparent difficulty is reconciled in this way. The holy soul is a soul with God; moving as God moves; doing as God does; looking as God looks. If, therefore, God is looking within us, as we may generally learn from the intimations of His providences, then it is a sign that we are to look within ourselves. Our little eye, our small and almost imperceptible ray, must look in, in the midst of the light of His great and burning eye. It is thus that we may inspect ourselves without a separation from God.

On the same principle, we may be watchful and careful over our neighbours; watching them, not in our own time, but in God's time; not in the censoriousness of nature, but in the kindness and forbearance of grace; not as separate from God, but in concurrence with Him.

Article twelve

The soul, in the state of pure love, acts in simplicity. Its inward rule of action is found in the decisions of a sanctified conscience. These decisions, based upon judgements that are free from self-interest, may not always be absolutely right, because our views and judgements, being limited, can extend only to things in part;

but they may be said to be relatively right: they conform to things so far as we are permitted to see them and understand them, and convey to the soul a moral assurance, that, when we act in accordance with them, we are doing as God would have us do. Such a conscience is enlightened by the Spirit of God; and when we act thus, under its Divine guidance, looking at what now is and not at what may be, looking at the right of things and not at their relations to our personal and selfish interests, we are said to act in simplicity. This is the true mode of action.

Article thirteen

Thus, in this singleness of spirit, we do things, as some experimental writers express it, without knowing what we do. We are so absorbed in the thing to be done, and in the importance of doing it rightly, that we forget ourselves. Perfect love has nothing to spare from its object for itself, and he who prays perfectly is never thinking how well he prays.

Holy souls are without impatience, but not without trouble; are above murmuring, but not above affliction. The souls of those who are thus wholly in Christ may be regarded in two points of view, or rather in two parts; namely, the natural appetites, propensities, and affections, on the one hand, which may be called the inferior part; and the judgement, the moral sense, and the will, on the other, which may be described as the superior part. As things are, in the present life, those who are wholly devoted to God may suffer in the inferior part, and may be at rest in the superior. Their wills may be in harmony with the Divine will; they may be approved in their judgements and conscience, and at the same time may suffer greatly in their physical relations, and in their natural sensibilities. In this manner, Christ upon the cross, while His will remained firm in its union with the will of His heavenly Father, suffered much through His physical system; He felt the painful longings of thirst, the pressure of the thorns, and the agony of the spear. He was deeply afflicted also for the friends He left behind Him, and for a dying world. But in His inner and higher nature, where He felt Himself sustained by the secret voice uttered in His sanctified conscience and in His unchangeable faith, He was peaceful and happy.

Article fourteen

A suitable repression of the natural appetites is profitable and necessary. We are told that the body should be brought into subjection. Those physical mortifications, therefore, which are instituted to this end, denominated austerities, are not to be disapproved. When practised within proper limits, they tend to correct evil habits, to preserve us against temptation, and to give self-control.

The practice of austerities, with the views and on the principles indicated, should be accompanied with the spirit of recollection, of love, and prayer. Christ Himself, whose retirement to solitary places, whose prayers and fastings are not to be forgotten, has given us the pattern which it is proper for us to follow. We must sometimes use force against our stubborn nature. 'Since the days of John, the kingdom of heaven suffers violence; and the violent take it by force.'

Article fifteen

The simple desire of our own happiness, kept in due subordination, is innocent. This desire is natural to us; and is properly denominated the principle of SELF-LOVE. When the principle of self-love passes its appropriate limit, it becomes selfishness. Self-love is innocent; selfishness is wrong. Selfishness was the sin of the first angel, 'who rested in himself', as St Augustine expresses it, instead of referring himself to God.

In many Christians a prominent principle of action is the desire of happiness. They love God and they love heaven; they love holiness, and they love the pleasures of holiness; they love to do good, and they love the rewards of doing good. This is well; but there is something better. Such Christians are inferior to those who forget the nothingness of the creature in the infinitude of the Creator, and love God for His own glory alone.

Article sixteen

No period of the Christian life is exempt from temptation. The temptations incident to the earlier stages are different from those incident to a later period, and are to be resisted in a different manner.

Sometimes the temptations concerning moving from mixed love to pure love are somewhat peculiar, being adapted to test whether we love God for Himself alone.

In the lower or mixed state the methods of resisting temptations are various. Sometimes the subject of these trials boldly faces them, and endeavours to overcome them by a direct resistance. Sometimes he turns and flees. But in the state of pure love, when the soul has become strong in the Divine contemplation, it is the common rule laid down by religious writers, that the soul should keep itself fixed upon God in the exercise of its holy love as at other times, as the most effectual way of resisting the temptation, which would naturally expand its efforts in vain upon a soul in that state.

Article seventeen

The will of God is the ultimate and only rule of action. God manifests His will in various ways. The will of God may in some cases be ascertained by the operations of the human mind, especially when under a religious or gracious guidance. But He reveals His will chiefly in His written word. And nothing can be declared to be the will of God, which is at variance with His written or revealed will, which may also be called His positive will.

If we sin, it is that God permits it; but it is also true, that He disapproves and condemns it as contrary to His immutable holiness.

It is the business of the sinner to repent. The state of penitence has temptations peculiar to itself. He is sometimes tempted to murmuring and rebellious feelings, as if he had been unjustly left of God. When penitence is true, and in the highest state, it is free from the variations of human passion.

Article eighteen

Among other distinctions of prayer, we may make that of vocal and silent, the prayer of the lips and the prayer of the affections. Vocal prayer, without the heart attending it, is superstitious and wholly unprofitable. To pray without recollection in God and without love, is to pray as the heathen did, who thought to be heard for the multitude of their words.

Nevertheless, vocal prayer, when attended by right affections, ought to be both recognized and encouraged, as being calculated to strengthen the thoughts and feelings it expresses, and to awaken new ones, and also for the reason that it was taught by the Son of God to His Apostles, and that it has been practised by the whole Church in all ages. To make light of this sacrifice of praise, this fruit of the lips, would be an impiety.

Silent prayer, in its common form, is also profitable. Each has its peculiar advantages, as each has its place.

There is also a modification of prayer, which may be termed the prayer of silence. This is a prayer too deep for words. The common form of silent prayer is voluntary. In the prayer of contemplative silence, the lips seem to be closed almost against the will.

Article nineteen
The principles of holy living extend to everything. For instance, in the matter of reading, he who has given himself wholly to God, can read only what God permits him to read. He cannot read books, however characterized by wit or power, merely to indulge an idle curiosity, or to please himself alone.

In reading this may be a suitable direction, namely, to read but little at a time, and to interrupt the reading by intervals of religious recollection, in order that we may let the Holy Spirit more deeply imprint in us Christian truths.

God, in the person of the Holy Ghost, becomes to the fully renovated mind the great inward Teacher. This is a great truth. At the same time we are not to suppose that the presence of the inward teacher exempts us from the necessity of the outward lesson. The Holy Ghost, operating through the medium of a purified judgement, teaches us by the means of books, especially by the word of God, which is never to be laid aside.

Article twenty
One characteristic of the lower states of religious experience is, that they are sustained, in a considerable degree, by meditative and reflective acts. As faith is comparatively weak and temptations are strong, it becomes necessary to gain strength by such meditative

and reflective acts, by the consideration of various truths applicable to their situation, and of the motives drawn from such truths. Accordingly, souls array before them all the various motives drawn from the consideration of misery on the one hand, and of happiness on the other; all the motives of fear and hope.

It is different with those who have given themselves wholly to God in the exercise of pure or perfect love. The soul does not find it necessary to delay and to meditate, in order to discover motives of action. It finds its motive of action a motive simple, uniform, peaceable, and still powerful beyond any other power, in its own principle of life.

Meditation, inquiry, and reasoning, are exceedingly necessary to the great body of Christians; and absolutely indispensable to those in the beginnings of the Christian life. To take away these helps would be to take away the child from the breast before it can digest solid food. Still they are only the props, and not the life itself.

Article twenty-one

'Whether, therefore,' says the Apostle, 'you eat or drink, or whatsoever you do, do all things to the glory of God' (1 Corinthians 10:31). And in another passage he says, 'Let all things be done with charity' (1 Corinthians 16:14). And again, 'By love serve one another' (Galatians 5:13): passages which, with many others, imply two things; first, that everything which is done by the Christian ought to be done from a holy principle; and, second, that this principle is love.

Article twenty-two

Our acceptance with God, when our hearts are wholly given to Him, does not depend upon our being in a particular state, but simply upon our being in that state in which God in His providence requires us to be. The doctrine of holiness, therefore, while it recognizes and requires, on its appropriate occasions, the prayer of contemplation or of contemplative silence, is not only not inconsistent with other forms of prayer, but is not at all inconsistent with the practice of the ordinary acts, duties, and virtues of life. It would be a great mistake to suppose, that a man who bears

the Saviour's image, is any the less on that account a good neighbour or a good citizen; that he can think less or work less when
he is called to it; or that he is not characterized by the various
virtues, appropriate to our present situation, of temperance, truth,
forbearance, forgiveness, kindness, chastity, justice. There is a law,
involved in the very nature of holiness, which requires it to adapt
itself to every variety of situation.

Article twenty-three

It is in accordance with the views of Dionysius the Areopagite, to
say that the holy soul in its contemplative state, is occupied with
the pure or spiritual Divinity. That is to say, it is occupied with
God, in distinction from any mere image of God, such as could
be addressed to the touch, the sight, or any of the senses.

And this is not all. It does not satisfy the desires of the soul in
its contemplative state, to occupy itself merely with the attributes
of God; with His power, wisdom, goodness, and the like; but it
rather seeks and unites itself with the God of the attributes. The
attributes of God are not God himself. The power of God is not
an identical expression with the God of power; nor is the wisdom
of God identical with the God of wisdom. The holy soul, in its
contemplative state, loves to unite itself with God, considered as
the subject of His attributes. It is not infinite wisdom, infinite
power, or infinite goodness, considered separately from the existence of whom they can be predicated, which it loves and adores;
but the God of infinite wisdom, power, and goodness.

Article twenty-four

Christ is 'the way, and the truth, and the life'. The grace which
sanctifies as well as that which justifies, is by Him and through
Him. He is the true and living way; and no man can gain the
victory over sin, and be brought into union with God, without
Christ. And when, in some mitigated sense, we may be said to
have arrived at the end of the way by being brought home to the
Divine fold and reinstated in the Divine image, it would be sad
indeed if we should forget the way itself, as Christ is sometimes
called. At every period of our progress, however advanced it may

be, our life is derived from God through Him and for Him. The most advanced souls are those which are most possessed with the thoughts and the presence of Christ.

Any other view would be extremely pernicious. It would be to snatch from the faithful eternal life, which consists in knowing the only true God and Jesus Christ His Son, whom He has sent.

Article twenty-five
The way of holiness is wonderful, but it is not miraculous. Those in it, walk by simple faith alone. And perhaps there is nothing more remarkable nor wonderful in it, than that a result so great should be produced by a principle so simple.

When people have arrived at the state of divine union, so that, in accordance with the prayer of the Saviour, they are made one with Christ in God, they no longer seem to put forth distinct inward acts, but their state appears to be characterized by a deep and Divine repose.

The continuous act is the act of faith, which brings into moral and religious union with the Divine nature; faith which, through the plenitude of Divine grace, is kept firm, unbroken.

The appearance of absolute continuity and unity in this blessed state is increased perhaps by the entire freedom of the mind from all eager, anxious, unquiet acts. The soul is not only at unity with itself in the respects which have been mentioned, but it has also a unity of rest.

This state of continuous faith and of consequent repose in God is sometimes denominated the passive state. The soul, at such times, ceases to originate acts which precede the grace of God. The decisions of her consecrated judgement, are the voice of the Holy Ghost in the soul. But if she first listens passively, it is subsequently her business to yield an active and effective co-operation in the line of duty which they indicate. The more pliant and supple the soul is to the Divine suggestions, the more real and efficacious is her own action, though without any excited and troubled movement. The more a soul receives from God, the more she ought to restore to Him of what she has from Him. This ebbing and flowing, if one may so express it, this communication on the part of God and the correspondent action on the part of man, constitute the order of grace on the one hand, and the action and fidelity of the creature on the other.

Article twenty-six

It would be a mistake to suppose, that the highest state of inward experience is characterized by great excitements, by raptures and ecstasies, or by any movements of feeling which would be regarded as particularly extraordinary.

One of the remarkable results in a soul of which faith is the sole governing principle, is, that it is entirely peaceful. Nothing disturbs it. And being thus peaceful, it reflects distinctly and clearly the image of Christ; like the placid lake, which shows, in its own clear and beautiful bosom, the exact forms of the objects around and above it. Another is, that having full faith in God and divested of all selfishness and resistance in itself, it is perfectly accessible and pliable to all the impressions of grace.

Article twenty-seven

It does not follow that those who possess the graces of a truly sanctified heart, are at liberty to reject the ordinary methods and rules of perception and judgement. They exercise and value wisdom, while they reject the selfishness of wisdom. The rules of holy living would require them every moment to make a faithful use of all the natural light of reason, as well as the higher and spiritual light of grace.

A holy soul values and seeks wisdom, but does not seek it in an unholy and worldly spirit. Nor, when it is made wise by the Spirit of wisdom, who dwells in all hearts that are wholly devoted to God, does it turn back from the giver to the gift, and rejoice in its wisdom as its own.

The wisdom of the truly holy soul is a wisdom which estimates things in the present moment. It judges of duty from the facts which now are; including, however, those things which have a relation to the present. It is an important remark, that the present moment necessarily possesses a moral extension; so that, in judging of it, we are to include all those things which have a natural and near relation to the thing actually in hand. It is in this manner that the holy soul lives in the present, committing the past to God, and leaving the future with that approaching hour which shall convert it into the present. 'Sufficient to the day is the evil thereof.' Tomorrow will take care of itself; it will bring, at its coming, its appropriate grace and light. When we live thus, God will not fail to give us our daily bread.

Such souls draw on themselves the special protection of Providence, under whose care they live, without a far extended and unquiet forecast, like little children resting in the bosom of their mother. Conscious of their own limited views, and keeping in mind the direction of the Saviour, Judge not that you be not judged, they are slow to pass judgement upon others. They are willing to receive reproof and correction; and, separate from the will of God, they have no choice or will of their own in anything.

These are the children whom Christ permits to come near Him. They combine the prudence of the serpent with the simplicity of the dove. But they do not appropriate their prudence to themselves as their own prudence, any more than they appropriate to themselves the beams of the natural sun, when they walk in its light.

These are the poor in spirit, whom Christ Jesus hath declared blessed; and who are as much taken off from any complacency in what others might call their merits, as all Christians ought to be from their temporal possessions. They are the 'little ones', to whom God is well pleased to reveal His mysteries, while He hides them from the wise and prudent.

Article twenty-eight
It is the doctrine of Augustine, as also of Thomas Aquinas, that the principle of holy love existing in the heart, necessarily includes in itself, or implies the existence of, all other Christian virtues. He who loves God with all his heart, will not violate the laws of purity, because it would be a disregard of the will of God, which he loves above all things. His love, under such circumstances, becomes the virtue of chastity. He has too much love and reverence for the will of God to murmur or repine under the

dispensations of His providence. His love, under such circumstances, becomes the virtue of patience. And thus this love becomes by turns, on their appropriate occasions, all the virtues. As his love is perfect, so the virtues which flow out of it, and are modified from it, will not be less so.

It is a maxim in the doctrines of holiness, that the holy soul is crucified to its own virtues, although it possesses them in the highest degree. The meaning of this saying is this: The holy soul is so crucified to self in all its forms, that it practises the virtues without taking complacency in its virtues as its own, and even without thinking how virtuous it is.

Article twenty-nine

The Apostle Paul speaks of Christians as dead. 'You are dead,' he says, 'and your life is hid with Christ in God' (Colossians 3:3). These expressions will apply, in their full import, only to those Christians who are in the state of unselfish or pure love. Their death is a death to selfishness. They are dead to pride and jealousy, self-seeking and envy, to malice, inordinate love of their own reputation, anything and everything which constitutes the fallen and vitiated life of nature. They have a new life, which is 'hid with Christ in God'.

The holy soul may be said to be united with God, without anything intervening or producing a separation, in three particulars.

First, it is thus united intellectually; that is to say, not by any idea which is based upon the senses, and which of course could give only a material image of God, but by an idea which is internal and spiritual in its origin, and makes God known to us as a Being without form.

Second, the soul is thus united to God, if we may so express it, affectionately. That is to say, when its affections are given to God, not indirectly through a self-interested motive, but simply because He is what He is. The soul is united to God in love without anything intervening, when it loves Him for His own sake.

Third, the soul is thus united to God practically; and this is the case when it does the will of God, not by simply following a prescribed form, but from the constantly operative impulse of holy love.

Article thirty

The doctrine of pure love has been known and recognized as a true doctrine among the truly contemplative and devout in all ages of the Church. The doctrine, however, has been so far above the common experience, that the pastors and saints of all ages have exercised a degree of discretion and care in making it known, except to those to whom God had already given both the attraction and light to receive it. Acting on the principle of giving milk to infants and strong meat to those that were more advanced, they addressed in the great body of Christians the motives of fear and of hope, founded on the consideration of happiness or of misery. It seemed to them, that the motive of God's glory, in itself considered, a motive which requires us to love God for Himself alone without a distinct regard and reference to our own happiness, could be profitably addressed, as a general rule, only to those who are somewhat advanced in inward experience.

Article thirty-one

Among the various forms of expression indicative of the highest experience, we sometimes find that of 'Divine union', or 'union with God'.

Union with God, not a physical but moral or religious union, necessarily exists in souls that are in the state of pure love. The state of 'Divine union' is not a higher state than that of pure love, but may rather be described as the same state.

Strive after it; but do not too readily or easily believe that you have attained to it. The traveller, after many fatigues and dangers, arrives at the top of a mountain. As he looks abroad from that high eminence, and in that clear atmosphere, he sees his native city; and it seems to him to be very near. Overjoyed at the sight, and perhaps deceived by his position, he proclaims himself as already at the end of his journey. But he soon finds that the distance was greater than he supposed. He is obliged to descend into valleys, and to climb over hills, and to surmount rugged rocks, and to wind his tired steps over many a mile of weary way, before he reaches that home and city, which he once thought so near.

It is thus in relation to the sanctification of the heart. True holiness of heart is the object at which the Christian aims. He beholds it before him, as an object of transcendent beauty, and as perhaps near at hand. But as he advances towards it, he finds the way longer and more difficult than he had imagined. But if on the one hand we should be careful not to mistake an intermediate stopping place for the end of the way, we should be equally careful on the other not to be discouraged by the difficulties we meet with; remembering that the obligation to be holy is always binding upon us, and that God will help those who put their trust in Him.

'Whatsoever is born of God, overcomes the world; and this is the victory that overcomes the world, EVEN OUR FAITH' (1 John 5:4).

Take Time

Author unknown
Take time to think: it is the source of power.
Take time to play: it is the secret of perpetual youth.
Take time to read: it is the fountain of wisdom.
Take time to pray: it is the greatest power on earth.
Take time to love and be loved: it is a God-given privilege.
Take time to be friendly: it is the road to happiness.
Take time to laugh: it is the music of the soul.
Take time to give: it is too short a day to be selfish.
Take time to work: it is the price of success.
Take time to do charity: it is the key to heaven.

The seeds of success

Author unknown

God, I thank you for this day,

I know I have not accomplished as yet all You expect of me, and if that is Your reason for bathing me in the fresh dew of another day, I am most grateful.

I am prepared, at last, to make You proud of me.

I will forget yesterday, with all its trials and tribulations, aggravations and setbacks, angers and frustrations. The past is already a dream from which I can neither retrieve a single word nor erase any foolish deeds.

I will resolve, however, that if I have injured anyone yesterday through my thoughtlessness, I will not let this day's sun set before I make amends, and nothing I do today will be of greater importance.

I will not fret the future. My success and happiness does not depend on straining to see what lurks dimly on the horizon but to do, this day, what lies clearly at hand.

I will treasure this day, for it's all I have. I know that its rushing hours cannot be accumulated or stored, like precious grain, for future use.

I will live as all good actors do when they are onstage – only in the moment. I cannot perform at my best today by regretting my previous act's mistakes or worrying about the scene to come.

I will embrace today's difficult tasks, take off my coat, and make dust in the world. I will remember that the busier I am, the less harm I am apt to suffer, the tastier will be my food, the sweeter my sleep, and the better satisfied I will be with my place in the world.

I will free myself today from slavery to the clock and calendar. Although I will plan this day in order to conserve my steps and energy, I will begin to measure my life in deeds, not years; in thoughts, not seasons; in feelings, not figures on a dial.

I will remain aware of how little it takes to make this a happy day. Never will I pursue happiness, because it is not a goal, just a by-product, and there is no happiness in having or in getting, only in giving.

I will run from no danger I might encounter today, because I am certain that nothing will happen to me that I am not equipped to handle with Your help. Just as any gem is polished by friction, I am certain to become more valuable through this day's adversities, and if You close one door, You always open another for me.

I will live this day as if it were Christmas. I will be a giver of gifts and deliver to my enemies the gifts of forgiveness; my opponents, tolerance; my friends, a smile; my children, a good example, and every gift will be wrapped with unconditional love.

I will not waste even a precious second today in anger or hate or jealousy or selfishness. I know that the seeds I sow I will harvest, because every action, good or bad, is always followed by an equal reaction. I will plant only good seeds this day.

I will treat today as a priceless violin. One may draw harmony from it and another, discord, yet no one will blame the instrument. Life is the same, and if I play it correctly, it will give forth beauty, but if I play it ignorantly, it will produce ugliness.

I will condition myself to look on every problem I encounter today as no more than a pebble in my shoe. I remember the pain so harsh I could hardly walk, and recall my surprise when I removed my shoe and found only a grain of sand.

I will work convinced that nothing great was ever achieved without enthusiasm. To do anything today that is truly worth doing, I must not stand back shivering and thinking of the cold and danger, but jump in with gusto and scramble through as well as I can.

I will face the world with goals set for this day, but they will be attainable ones, not the vague, impossible variety declared by those who make a career of failure. I realize that You always try me with a little, first, to see what I would do with a lot.

I will not hide my talents. If I am silent, I am forgotten; if I do not advance, I will fall back; if I walk away from any challenge today, my self-esteem will be forever scarred; and if I cease to grow, even a little, I will become smaller. I reject the stationary position because it is always the beginning of the end.

I will keep a smile on my face and in my heart, even when it hurts today. I know that the world is a looking glass and gives back to me the reflection of my own soul. Now I understand the secret of correcting the attitude of others and that is to correct my own.

I will turn away from any temptation today that might cause me to break my word or lose my self-respect. I am positive that the only thing I possess more valuable than my life is my honour.

I will work this day with all my strength, content in the knowledge that life does not consist of wallowing in the past or peering anxiously at the future. It is appalling to contemplate the great number of painful steps by which one arrives at a truth so old, so obvious, and so frequently expressed. Whatever it offers, little or much, my life is now.

I will pause whenever I am feeling sorry for myself today, and remember that this is the only day I have and must play it to the fullest. What my part may signify in the great whole, I may not recognize, but I am here to play it and now is the time.

I will count this day a separate life. I will remember that those who have fewest regrets are those who take each moment as it comes for all that it is worth.

This is my day! These are my seeds. Thank you God, for this precious garden of time.

PART TWO

THE
DEVOTIONAL LIFE

Abiding

A growing communion

Samuel Rutherford

I urge upon you communion with Christ, a growing communion.

Set us on fire

Augustine

Come, Lord,
work on us,
set us on fire
and clasp us close,
be fragrant to us,
draw us to your love,
let us run to you.

Clothe me with yourself

Catherine of Siena

Clothe me, clothe me with yourself, eternal truth, so that I may live this earthly life with true obedience, and with the light of your most holy faith.

My spirit longs for Thee

John Byrom

My spirit longs for Thee
Within my troubled breast,
Though I unworthy be
Of so divine a guest.

Of so divine a guest
Unworthy though I be,
Yet has my heart no rest
Unless it come from thee.

Come, my Way, my Truth, my Life

George Herbert

Come, my Way, my Truth, my Life:
Such a Way as gives us breath:
Such a Truth as ends of strife:
Such a Life as killeth death.
Come, my Light, my Feast, my Strength:
Such a Light, as shows a feast:
Such a Feast, as mends in length:
Such a Strength, as makes his guest.
Come, my Joy, my Love, my Heart:
Such a Joy, as none can move:
Such a Love, as none can part:
Such a Heart, as joys in love.

Therefore give us love

Christopher Wordsworth

Love is kind and suffers long,
Love is meek and thinks no wrong,

Love than death itself more strong;
Therefore give us love.

Faith will vanish into sight;
Hope be emptied in delight;
Love in heaven will shine more bright;
Therefore give us love.

May the love of Jesus fill me

K.B. Wilkinson
May the mind of Christ my Saviour
Live in me from day to day,
By his love and power controlling
All I do and say.

May the word of God dwell richly
In my heart from hour to hour,
So that all may see I triumph
Only through his power.

May the love of Jesus fill me
As the waters fill the sea;
Him exalting, self abasing,
This is victory.

I rest my weary soul in thee

George Matheson
O Love that wilt not let me go,
I rest my weary soul in thee;
I give thee back the life I owe,
That in thine ocean depths its flow
May richer, fuller be.

Our hearts are restless

Augustine

Almighty God, in whom we live and move and have our being, you have made us for yourself and our hearts are restless until in you they find their rest. Grant us purity of heart and strength of purpose, that no selfish passion may hinder us from knowing your will, no weakness from doing it; but that in your light we may see light clearly, and in your service we may find our perfect freedom; through Jesus Christ our Lord.

Praise and Thanksgiving
Blessed are you, O Lord

David, 1 Chronicles 29:10–11 NRSV

Blessed are you, O Lord, the God of our ancestor Israel, for ever and ever. Yours, O Lord, are the greatness, the power, the glory, the victory, and the majesty; for all that is in the heavens and on the earth is yours; yours is the kingdom, O Lord, and you are exalted as head above all.

Te Deum Laudamus

Author unknown, fourth century

We praise thee, O God, we acknowledge thee to be the Lord.
All the earth doth worship thee, the Father everlasting.
To thee all angels cry aloud, the heavens and all the powers therein;
To thee cherubim and seraphim continually do cry,
Holy, holy, holy, Lord God of Sabaoth:
Heaven and earth are full of the majesty of thy glory.
The glorious company of the apostles praise thee.
The goodly fellowship of the prophets praise thee.
The noble army of martyrs praise thee.
The holy church throughout the world doth acknowledge thee,
The Father of an infinite majesty;

Thine adorable, true and only Son;
Also the Holy Ghost, the Comforter.

Thou art the King of glory, O Christ;
Thou art the everlasting Son of the Father.
When thou tookest upon thee to deliver man
Thou didst humble thyself to be born of a virgin.
When thou hadst overcome the sharpness of death
Thou didst open the kingdom of heaven to all believers.
Thou sittest at the right hand of God in the glory of the Father.
We believe that thou shalt come to be our judge.
We therefore pray thee help thy servants
whom thou hast redeemed with thy precious blood.
Make them to be numbered with thy saints in glory everlasting.

All people that on earth do dwell

William Kethe

All people that on earth do dwell,
  Sing to the Lord with cheerful voice;
Him serve with mirth, his praise forth tell,
  Come ye before him, and rejoice.

The Lord, ye know, is God indeed;
  Without our aid he did us make;
We are his folk, he doth us feed,
  And for his sheep he doth us take.

O enter then his gates with praise,
  Approach with joy his courts unto;
Praise, laud, and bless his name always.
  For it is seemly so to do.

For why, the Lord our God is good;
   His mercy is for ever sure;
His truth at all times firmly stood,
   And shall from age to age endure.

Praise to the Holiest in the height

J.H. Newman

Praise to the Holiest in the height,
   And in the depth be praise;
In all his words most wonderful,
   Most sure in all his ways.

O loving wisdom of our God!
   When all was sin and shame,
A second Adam to the fight
   And to the rescue came.

O wisest love! that flesh and blood,
   Which did in Adam fail,
Should strive afresh against the foe,
   Should strive and should prevail.

And that a higher gift than grace
   Should flesh and blood refine,
God's presence and his very self,
   And essence all-divine.

O generous love! That he who smote
   In Man, for man, the foe,
The double agony in Man,
   For man, should undergo;

And in the garden secretly,
  And on the cross on high,
Should teach his brethren, and inspire
  To suffer and to die.

Praise to the Holiest in the height,
  And in the depth be praise;
In all his words most wonderful,
  Most sure in all his ways.

You are holy, Lord

Francis of Assisi

You are holy, Lord, the only God,
and your deeds are wonderful.
You are strong.
You are great.
You are the most high.
You are almighty.
You, holy Father, are King of heaven and earth.
You are three and one, Lord God, all Good.
You are Good, all Good, supreme Good,
Lord God, living and true.
You are love. You are wisdom.
You are humility. You are endurance.
You are rest. You are peace.
You are joy and gladness.
You are justice and moderation.
You are all our riches, and you suffice for us.
You are beauty.
You are gentleness.
You are our protector.
You are our guardian and defender.
You are our courage. You are our haven and our hope.
You are our faith, our great consolation.

You are our eternal life, great and wonderful Lord,
God almighty, merciful Saviour.

Prayer
It is not necessary to be always at church

Brother Lawrence

It will be of great importance if you can leave the care of
your affairs to, and spend the remainder of your life only in
worshipping God. He requires no great matters of us; a little
remembrance of Him from time to time, a little adoration:
sometimes to pray for His grace, sometimes to offer Him your
sufferings, and sometimes to return Him thanks for the favours
He has given you, and still gives you, in the midst of your troubles, and to console yourself with Him the oftenest you can. Lift
up your heart to Him, sometimes even at your meals, and when
you are in company: the least little remembrance will always be
acceptable to Him. You need not cry very loud; He is nearer to
us than we are aware of.

It is not necessary for being with God to be always at church;
we may make an oratory of our heart, wherein to retire from time
to time, to converse with Him in meekness, humility, and love.
Every one is capable of such familiar conversation with God,
some more, some less: He knows what we can do. Let us begin
then; perhaps He expects but one generous resolution on our
part. Have courage. We have but little time to live; you are near
sixty-four, and I am almost eighty. Let us live and die with God:
sufferings will be sweet and pleasant to us, while we are with
Him: and the greatest pleasures will be, without Him, a cruel
punishment to us. May He be blessed for all. Amen.

Use yourself then by degrees thus to worship Him, to beg His
grace, to offer Him your heart from time to time, in the midst of
your business, even every moment if you can. Do not always
scrupulously confine yourself to certain rules, or particular forms
of devotion; but act with a general confidence in God, with love
and humility.

A short prayer

William Langland
A short prayer finds its way to heaven.

Prayer is the Christian's vital breath

James Montgomery
Prayer is the soul's sincere desire,
Uttered or unexpressed;
The motion of a hidden fire,
That trembles in the breast.

Prayer is the burden of a sigh,
The falling of a tear,
The upward glance of an eye
Where none but God is near.

Prayer is the simplest form of speech
That infant lips can try;
Prayer the sublimest strains that reach
The majesty on high.

Prayer is the contrite sinner's voice
Returning from his ways,
While angels in their songs rejoice,
And cry, 'Behold, he prays'.

Prayer is the Christian's vital breath,
The Christian's native air,
His watchword at the gates of death:
He enters heaven with prayer.

'Holy, holy, holy'

Francis of Assisi

Francis of Assisi used this collection of Bible verses, given here in the
NRSV, for the praise of God.

'Holy, holy, holy, the Lord God the Almighty, who was and is and
is to come' (Revelation 4:8).

'You are worthy, our Lord and God, to receive glory and honour
and power, for you created all things, and by your will they existed and were created' (Revelation 4:11).

'Worthy is the Lamb that was slaughtered to receive power and
wealth and wisdom and might and honour and glory and blessing!' (Revelation 5:12).

Let us bless the Father, the Son and the Holy Spirit. Praise him
and exult him above all for ever.
    'Praise our God, all you his servants, and all who fear him, small
and great' (Revelation 19:5).

Let 'every creature in heaven and on earth, and under the earth
and in the sea, and all that is in them, [praise God] singing, "To the
one seated on the throne and to the Lamb be blessing and honour and glory and might for ever and ever!"' (Revelation 5:13).
    Glory be to the Father, and to the Son, and to the Holy Spirit.
Praise him and exalt him above all for ever. As it was in the beginning, is now, and ever shall be, world without end. Amen. Praise
him and exalt him above all for ever.

A cell in her heart

E.B. Pusey

Catherine of Siena made a cell in her heart. Afterwards, in a most busy life she could keep quite close to God and without the least distraction.

Wandering thoughts

Brother Lawrence

Concerning wandering thoughts in prayer

You tell me nothing new: you are not the only one that is troubled with wandering thoughts. Our mind is extremely roving; but as the will is mistress of all our faculties, she must recall them, and carry them to God, as their last end.

When the mind, for want of being sufficiently reduced by recollection, at our first engaging in devotion, has contracted certain bad habits of wandering and dissipation, they are difficult to overcome, and commonly draw us, even against our wills, to the things of the earth.

I believe one remedy for this is, to confess our faults, and to humble ourselves before God. I do not advise you to use multiplicity of words in prayer; many words and long discourses being often the occasions of wandering: hold yourself in prayer before God, like a dumb or paralytic beggar at a rich man's gate: let it be your business to keep your mind in the presence of the Lord. If it sometimes wander, and withdraw itself from Him, do not much disquiet yourself for that; trouble and disquiet serve rather to distract the mind, than to recollect it; the will must bring it back in tranquillity; if you persevere in this manner, God will have pity on you.

One way to recollect the mind easily in the time of prayer, and preserve it more in tranquillity, is not to let it wander too far at other times: you should keep it strictly in the presence of God; and being accustomed to think of Him often, you will find it easy

to keep your mind calm in the time of prayer, or at least to recall
it from its wanderings.

Where and when to pray

Joseph Hall

Solitariness of place is the most appropriate place for meditation.
Retire from other people, if you want to talk with profit with
yourself. So Jesus meditates alone on the mount; Isaac, in the fields;
John the Baptist, in the desert; David, on his bed; Chrysostom, in
the bath: each, in different places; but all solitary. Nowhere is free
of God's presence, he is not tied to any single place. Some people
find their own room best, since their eyes can wander no further
than the walls and so help to keep in check their wandering
thoughts. Other people find their souls are more free as they
behold God's heaven above them and around them. So long as you
are alone and quiet it does not matter where you are.

No one time for praying can be prescribed for everyone;
neither is God limited to set times and people differ among
themselves when they find it best to pray. Some people find the
golden hours of the morning the best for meditation. Then the
body is fresh and calm from resting, and the soul has not yet had
time to be distracted by outward things. Other people find that
they can best learn wisdom at night. Like Job, they hope that their
bed will bring them comfort in their meditation. They are tired
of earthly cares and are ready to appreciate and love heavenly
things. I, personally, have found Isaac's time best, when he went
out in the evening to meditate. But no habit belonging to another
is necessarily best suited to another person. All that matters is that
we set ourselves a time to pray and then set apart that time, when
we are best able to serve God in this way.

To pray in the Holy Spirit

William Gurnall

To pray in the Spirit is the inward principle of prayer. It comprehends both the spirit of the person praying, and the Spirit of God by which our spirits are fitted for, and acted in, prayer.

Groans

John Bunyan

The best prayers have more often groans than words.

Give us, we beseech Thee, love

St Columba

O Lord, give us, we beseech Thee, in the name of Jesus Christ Thy Son our Lord, that love which can never cease, that will kindle our lamps but not extinguish them, that they may burn in us and enlighten others.

Do Thou, O Christ, our dearest Saviour, Thyself kindle our lamps that they may evermore shine in Thy Temple and receive unquenchable light from Thee, that will enlighten our darkness and lessen the darkness of the world.

The Church's banquet

George Herbert

Prayer, the Church's banquet, Angels' age,
  God's breath in man returning to his birth,
  The soul in paraphrase, heart in pilgrimage,
The Christian plummet, sounding heaven and earth;
Engine against the Almighty, sinner's tower,
  Reversèd thunder, Christ-side-piercing spear,
  The six-days' world transposing in an hour,

A kind of tune, which all things hear and fear;
Softness, and peace, and joy, and love, and bliss,
　　Exalted manna, gladness of the best,
　　.　*Heaven in ordinary, man well drest,*
The milky way, the bird of Paradise,
　　Church-bells beyond the stars heard, the soul's blood,
　　The land of spices; something understood.

On his knees

Robert Murray M'Cheyne

What a man is on his knees before God, that he is – no more, no less.

Prayer is the ascent of the mind to God

Jeremy Taylor

Prayer is the ascent of the mind to God. It is an abstract and sum-mary of Christian religion. Prayer is an act of religion and divine worship, confessing His power and His mercy; it celebrates His attributes, and confesses His glories, and reveres His Person, and implores His aid, and gives thanks for His blessings; it is an act of humility, condescension, and dependence, expressed in the pros-tration of our bodies and humiliation of our spirits; it is an act of charity, when we pray for others; it is an act of repentance, when it confesses and begs pardon for our sins, and exercises every grace according to the design of the man, and the matter of the prayer.

Our common supplications

John Chrysostom

Almighty God, who hast given us grace at this time with one accord to make our common supplications unto thee; and dost promise, that when two or three are gathered together in thy

Name thou wilt grant their requests; Fulfil now, O Lord, the
desires and petitions of thy servants, as may be most expedient for
them; granting us in this world knowledge of thy truth, and in the
world to come life everlasting. Amen.

The first rule of right prayer

John Calvin

The first rule of right prayer is to have our heart and mind framed
as becomes those who are entering into converse with God.

Pray for my soul

Alfred, Lord Tennyson

More things are wrought by prayer than this world dreams of.
Therefore, let thy voice rise like a fountain for me night and day.
For what are men better than sheep or goats that nourish a blind
life within the brain, if, knowing God, they lift not hands of
prayer both for themselves and those who call them friend?

A ladder to God

Augustine

What can be more excellent than prayer; what is more profitable
to our life; what sweeter to our souls; what more sublime, in the
course of our whole life, than the practice of prayer!

He whose attitude towards Christ is correct does indeed ask 'in
his name' and receives what he asks for, if it is something which
does not stand in the way of his salvation. He gets it, however,
only when he ought to receive it, for certain things are not
refused us, but their granting is delayed to a fitting time.

Holy prayer is the column of all virtues; a ladder to God; the
support of widows; the foundation of faith; the crown of religious; the sweetness of the married life.

Prayer is the protection of holy souls; a consolation for the guardian angel; an insupportable torment to the devil; a most acceptable homage to God; the best and most perfect praise for penitents and religious; the greatest honour and glory; the preserver of spiritual health.

Confidence in God

Francis de Sales

It is good to mistrust ourselves, but how would that advantage us were we not to throw all our confidence on God, and to wait on His mercy? If you feel no such confidence, cease not on that account from making these acts and from saying to Our Lord: 'Yet, O Lord, though I have no feeling of confidence in You, nevertheless, I know that You are my God, that I am all Yours, and that I have no hope but in Your goodness; so, I abandon myself entirely into Your Hands.' It is always in our power to make these acts; although we have difficulty in performing them, still there is no impossibility. Thus we testify faithfulness to our Lord.

Bible Reading
Holy Scripture: the fountain of truth

Homilies

There can be nothing either more necessary or profitable, than the knowledge of Holy Scripture. And there is no truth nor doctrine, necessary for our justification and everlasting salvation, but that is, or may be, drawn out of that fountain and well of truth.

The Bible and salvation

William Beveridge, Ecclesia Anglicana Ecclesia Catholica, 1716
This Holy Scripture, thus written in Hebrew and Greek, in those languages wherein it was written, containeth nothing but the will

of God and the whole will of God; so that there is nothing necessary to be believed concerning God, nor done in obedience
unto God by us, but what is here revealed to us; and therefore all
traditions of men which are contrary to this word of God are
necessarily to be abhorred, and all traditions of men not recorded
in this word of God are not necessarily to be believed. What is
here written we are bound to believe because it is written; and
what is not here written we are not bound to believe because it
is not written. I say we are not bound to believe it, but I cannot
say we are bound not to believe it; for there be many truths which
we may believe, nay, are bound to believe, because truth, which
notwithstanding are not recorded in the word of God. But
though there be many things we may believe, yet there is nothing we need believe in order to our everlasting happiness which
is not here written; so that if we believe all that is here spoken,
and do all that is here commanded, we shall certainly be saved,
though we do not believe what is not here spoken, nor do what
is not here commanded.

Authority and tradition

James Ussher

To begin ... with traditions, which is your forlorn hope that in the
first place we are to set upon, this must I needs tell you before we
begin, that you much mistake the matter if you think that traditions of all sorts promiscuously are struck at by our religion. We
willingly acknowledge that the Word of God, which by some of
the Apostles was set down in writing, was both by themselves and
others of their fellow-labourers delivered by word of mouth; and
that the Church in succeeding ages was bound, not only to preserve those sacred writings committed to her trust, but also to
deliver unto her children, *viva voce*, the form of wholesome words
contained therein. Traditions, therefore, of this nature come not
within the compass of our controversy; the question being
betwixt us *de ipsa doctrina tradita*, not *de tradendi modo*, touching
the substance of the doctrine delivered, not of the manner of

delivering it. Again, it must be remembered that here we speak of the doctrine delivered as the Word of God, that is, on points of religion revealed unto the Prophets and Apostles for the perpetual information of God's people, not of rites and ceremonies and other ordinances which are left to the disposition of the Church, and consequently be not of Divine but of positive and human right. Traditions, therefore, of this kind likewise are not properly brought within the circuit of this question.

But that traditions of men should be obtruded unto us for articles of religion and admitted for parts of God's worship; or that any traditions should be accepted for parcels of God's Word, beside the Holy Scriptures and such doctrines as are either expressly therein contained or by sound inference may be deduced from thence, I think we have reason to gainsay; as long as for the first we have this direct sentence from God Himself, 'In vain do they worship Me, teaching for doctrines the commandments of men'; and for the second, the express warrant of the Apostle in the third chapter of the Second to Timothy, testifying of the Holy Scriptures, not only that they 'are able to make us wise unto salvation' (which they should not be able to do if they did not contain all things necessary to salvation), but also that by them 'the man of God', that is the minister of God's Word unto whom it appertaineth 'to declare all the counsel of God', may be 'perfectly instructed to every good work'; which could not be if the Scriptures did not contain all the counsel of God which was fit for him to learn, or if there were any other word of God which he were bound to teach that should not be contained within the limits of the Book of God.

Now whether herein we disagree from the doctrine generally received by the Fathers, we refer ourselves to their own sayings. For ritual traditions unwritten, and for doctrinal traditions, written indeed, but preserved also by the continual preaching of the pastors of the Church successively, we find no man a more earnest advocate than Tertullian. Yet he, having to deal with Hermogenes the heretic in a question concerning the faith, whether all things at the beginning were made of nothing, presseth him in this manner with the argument *ab authoritate* negative; for avoiding whereof the Papists are driven to fly for succour to their unwritten verities. 'Whether all things were made of any subject matter, I have as yet read nowhere. Let those of Hermogenes his shop shew that it is written. If it be not written, let them fear that Woe, which is allotted to such as add or take away.'

In the two Testaments, said Origen, 'every word that appertaineth to God may be required and discussed, and all knowledge of things out of them may be understood. But if anything do remain which the Holy Scripture doth not determine, no other third Scripture ought to be received for to authorize any knowledge, but that which remaineth we must commit to the fire, that is, we must reserve it to God. For in this present world, God would not have us to know all things.'

Hippolytus the Martyr, in his *Homily against the Heresy of Noetus*: 'There is one God, Whom we do not otherwise acknowledge, brethren, but out of the Holy Scriptures. For as he that would profess the wisdom of this world cannot otherwise attain hereunto, unless he read the doctrine of the philosophers, so whosoever of us will exercise piety toward God, cannot learn this elsewhere but out of the Holy Scriptures. Whatsoever, therefore, the Holy Scriptures do preach, that let us know; and whatsoever they teach, that let us understand.'

Athanasius, in his *Oration against the Gentiles*, toward the beginning: 'The Holy Scriptures given by inspiration of God are of themselves sufficient to the discovery of truth.'

St Ambrose: 'The things which we find not in the Scriptures, how can we use them?' And again: 'I read that he is the first, I read that he is not the second; they who say he is the second, let them shew it by reading.'

'It is well,' saith St Hilary, 'that thou art content with those things which be written.' And in another place he commendeth Constantius the Emperor for 'desiring the faith to be ordered only according to those things that be written'.

St Basil: 'Believe those things which are written; the things which are not written, seek not.' 'It is a manifest falling from the faith and an argument of arrogancy, either to reject any point of those things that are written, or to bring in any of those things that are not written.' He teacheth further 'that every word and action ought to be confirmed by the testimony of the Holy Scripture, for confirmation of the faith of the good, and the confusion of the evil'; and 'that it is the property of a faithful man to be fully persuaded of the truth of those things that are delivered in the Holy Scripture, and not to dare either to reject or to add anything thereunto. For if whatsoever is not of faith be sin, as the Apostle saith, and faith is by hearing and hearing by the Word of God, then whatsoever is without the Holy Scripture, being not of faith, must needs be sin.' Thus far St Basil.

In like manner, Gregory Nyssen, St Basil's brother, layeth this for a ground, 'which no man should contradict, that in that only the truth must be acknowledged wherein the seal of the Scripture testimony is to be seen'. And accordingly in another book, attributed also unto him, we find this conclusion made: 'Forasmuch as this is upholden with no testimony of the Scripture, as false we will reject it.'

Thus also St Hierome disputeth against Helvidius. 'As we deny not those things that are written, so we refuse those things that are not written. That God was born of a virgin, we believe, because we read it. That Mary did marry after she was delivered we believe not, because we read it not.'

'In those things,' saith St Augustine, 'which are laid down plainly in the Scriptures, all those things are found which appertain to faith and direction of life.' And again: 'Whatsoever ye hear from the Holy Scriptures, let that savour well unto you; whatsoever is without them, refuse, lest you wander in a cloud.' And in another place: 'All those things which in times past our ancestors have mentioned to be done toward mankind, and have delivered unto us, all those things also which we see and do deliver unto our posterity, so far as they appertain to the seeking and maintaining of true religion, the Holy Scripture hath not passed in silence.'

'The Holy Scripture,' said St Cyril of Alexandria, 'is sufficient to make them which are brought up in it wise and most approved, and furnished with most sufficient understanding.' And again, 'That which the Holy Scripture hath not said, by what means should we receive, and account it among these things that be true?'

Lastly, in the writings of Theodoret we meet with these kind of speeches. 'By the Holy Scripture alone am I persuaded.' 'I am not so bold as to affirm anything which the sacred Scripture passeth in silence.' 'It is an idle and a senseless thing to seek those things that are passed in silence.' 'We ought not to seek those things which are passed in silence, but rest in the things that are written.'

By the verdict of these twelve men you may judge what opinion was held in those ancient times of such traditions as did cross either the verity or the perfection of the sacred Scripture; which are the traditions we set ourselves against. Whereunto you may add, if you please, that remarkable sentence delivered by Eusebius Pamphili, in the name of the three hundred and eighteen fathers of the First General Council of Nice [Nicea]: 'Believe the things that are written; the things that are not written, neither think upon nor enquire after.'

The Bible and biblical research

Brooke Foss Westcott, The Bible in the Church, 1864

If [the Bible] is, as we devoutly believe, the very source and measure of our religious faith, it seems impossible to insist too earnestly on the supreme importance of patience, candour and truthfulness in investigating every problem which it involves ... And unless all past experience is worthless, the difficulties of the Bible are the most fruitful guides to its divine depths. It was said long since that 'God was pleased to leave difficulties upon the surface of scripture, that men might be forced to look below the surface.'

Contemplation and Meditation
Meditation and reading

Joseph Hall

We feed on what we read, but we digest only what we meditate of.

Meditation: the ladder of heaven

Joseph Hall

Meditation alone is the remedy of security and worldliness, and the pastime of saints, the ladder of heaven, and, in short, the best improvement of Christianity.

Prepare your mind for meditation

Robert Nelson, Meditations

In a religious sense, meditation is such an application of the mind to the consideration of any divine subject, as may best dispose us firmly to believe and embrace it, and stir up all the faculties of the soul to a vigorous execution of it. It consists in exciting holy movements in our souls, by virtue of those good thoughts we entertain and dwell on: and indeed without this practice the holy Scriptures and other devout books will have but little effect on us. For it is in this way that we digest what we read and turn it into nourishment for our minds.

Prepare your mind for this duty, by imploring God's assistance.

I firmly believe, O God, that thou art here, and everywhere present; that thy being and thy power is infinite. I adore thee with all humility as my sovereign Lord, and acknowledge that I am unworthy to appear before thee, because of my many sins; but for the sake of the blessed Jesus be gracious to me, and so enlighten my understanding, and influence my will and affections, that the present action may be to thy glory and for the good of my own soul.

Meditation and Prayer

Richard Rolle, The Fire of Love

God knows all things. He knows what we wish even before we ask for it. Yet we must pray, for many reasons. But first because Christ set us an example: he went up into the mountains alone at night to pray. And also because the apostles tell us to pray: 'Pray continually' (1 Thessalonians 5:17), and men ought always to pray and not give up (see Luke 18:1). But we ought to pray to acquire grace for this life and glory in the next. So we are told, 'For everyone who asks receives; he who seeks finds; and to him who knocks, the door will be opened' (Luke 11:10). Again, we pray because angels offer our prayers to God to help their fulfilment.

Thoughts and desires are indeed naked and open to God alone. Yet angels know when saints think worthy and holy things. They know when they are inflamed by the love of eternal life; God reveals it to them, and our outward acts display who serves God alone. That is why the angel said to Daniel, 'You are a man of strong desires' (Daniel 9:23, Vulgate). We should also pray because in constant prayer the soul is ignited with the fire of divine love. Our Lord speaks truly through the prophet, 'Is not my word like fire ... and like a hammer that breaks a rock in pieces?' (Jeremiah 23:29). And the psalmist says, 'Your speech is a burning fire' (Psalm 119:140, Vulgate).

Christian Belief
I am a Catholic Christian

King James I, A Premonition to All Most Mighty Monarchs, Kings, Free Princes, and States of Christendom, 1616

I will never be ashamed to render an account of my profession and of that hope that is in me, as the Apostle prescribeth. I am such a CATHOLIC CHRISTIAN as believeth the three Creeds, that of the Apostles, that of the Council of Nice [Nicea], and that of Athanasius ... and I believe them in that sense as the ancient Fathers and Councils that made them did understand them, to which three Creeds all the ministers of England do subscribe at their Ordination.

The Fathers

...As for the Fathers, I reverence them as much and more than the Jesuits do, and as much as themselves ever craved. For whatever the Fathers for the first five hundred years did with an unanimous consent agree upon, to be believed as a necessary point of salvation, I either will believe it also, or at least will be humbly silent, not taking upon me to condemn the same. But for every private Father's opinion, it binds not any conscience more than Bellarmine's, every one of the Fathers usually contradicting others. I will therefore in that case follow St Augustine's rule in judging of their opinions as I find them agree with the Scriptures. What I find agreeable thereto I will gladly embrace. What is otherwise I will (with their reverence) reject.

The Apocrypha

As for the Scriptures, no man doubteth I will believe them. But even for the Apocrypha, I hold them in the same manner that the ancients did. They are still printed and bound with our Bibles, and publicly read in our churches. I reverence them as the writings of holy and good men. But since they are not found in the Canon ... they are not sufficient alone to ground any Article of Faith, except it be confirmed by some other place of Canonical Scripture.

Saints

As for the Saints departed, I honour their memory, and in honour of them do we in our Church observe the days of so many of them as the Scripture doth canonize for saints; but I am loath to believe all the tales of the legended saints.

Images

I quarrel not with the making of images, either for public decoration or for men's private uses. But that they should be worshipped, be prayed to, or any holiness attributed unto them, was never known of the ancients. And the Scriptures are so directly, vehemently, and punctually against it, as I wonder what brain of man or suggestion of Satan durst offer it to Christians.

Seeking Forgiveness
Against you, you alone, have I sinned

Psalm 51:1–4, 10–11, 15–17 NRSV
Have mercy on me, O God,
*   according to your steadfast love;*
according to your abundant mercy
*   blot out my transgressions.*
Wash me thoroughly from my iniquity,
*   and cleanse me from my sin.*

For I know my transgressions,
*   and my sin is ever before me.*
Against you, you alone, have I sinned,
*   and done what is evil in your sight,*
so that you are justified in your sentence
*   and blameless when you pass judgement…*

Create in me a clean heart, O God,
*   and put a new and right spirit within me.*
Do not cast me away from your presence,
*   and do not take your holy spirit from me.*

O Lord, open my lips,
*   and my mouth will declare your praise.*
For you have no delight in sacrifice;
*   if I were to give a burnt-offering, you would not be pleased.*
The sacrifice acceptable to God is a broken spirit;
*   a broken and contrite heart, O God, you will not despise.*

Wilt Thou forgive?

John Donne
A Hymn to God the Father
Wilt Thou forgive that sin where I begun,
*   Which is my sin, though it were done before?*
Wilt Thou forgive that sin through which I run,
*   And do run still, though still I do deplore?*
*   When Thou hast done, Thou hast not done,*
*   For I have more.*

Wilt Thou forgive that sin which I have won
*   Others to sin? and made my sin their door?*
Wilt Thou forgive that sin which I did shun
*   A year or two, but wallowed in, a score?*
*   When Thou hast done, Thou hast not done,*
*   For I have more.*

I have a sin of fear, that when I have spun
*   My last thread, I shall perish on the shore;*
Swear by Thyself, that at my death Thy Son
*   Shall shine as He shines now and heretofore;*
*   And, having done that, Thou hast done,*
*   I fear no more.*

Thou wilt pardon me

Anne Brontë
Oppressed with sin and woe,
A burdened heart I bear;
Oppressed by many a mighty foe,
Yet I will not despair.

With this polluted heart,
I dare to come to thee —
Holy and mighty as thou art —
For thou wilt pardon me.

I feel that I am weak,
And prone to every sin;
But thou, who giv'st to those who seek,
Wilt give me strength within.

I need not fear my foes;
I need not yield to care;
I need not sink beneath my woes,
For thou wilt answer prayer.

In my Redeemer's name,
I give myself to thee;
And, all unworthy as I am,
My God will cherish me.

A Hymn

Phineas Fletcher
Drop, drop, slow tears,
*   And bathe those beauteous feet*
Which brought from Heaven
*   The news and Prince of Peace:*
Cease not, wet eyes,
*   His mercy to entreat;*
To cry for vengeance
*   Sin doth never cease.*
In your deep flood
*   Drown all my faults and fears;*
Nor let His eye
*   See sin, but through my tears.*

Have mercy on those who crave for your mercy

Thomas à Kempis

I offer up unto you my prayers and intercessions, for those especially who have in any way hurt, grieved, or found fault with me, or who have done me any harm or displeasure.

For all those also whom, at any time, I have annoyed, troubled, burdened, and scandalized, by words or deeds, knowingly or in ignorance: that you would grant us all equally pardon for our sins, and for our offences against each other.

Take away from our hearts, O Lord, all suspiciousness, indignation, anger and contention, and whatever may harm charity, and lessen brotherly love. Have mercy, O Lord, have mercy on those who crave for your mercy, give grace to those who stand in need of your grace, and make us such that we may be worthy to receive your grace, and go forward to life eternal.

Forgive them all for his sake

John Wesley
Forgive them all, O Lord:
our sins of omission and our sins of commission;
the sins of our youth and the sins of our riper years;
the sins of our souls and the sins of our bodies;
our secret and our more open sins;
our sins of ignorance and surprise,
and our more deliberate and presumptuous sins;
the sins we have done to please ourselves,
and the sins we have done to please others;
the sins we know and remember,
and the sins we have forgotten;
the sins we have striven to hide from others
and the sins by which we have offended others;
forgive them, O Lord, forgive them all for his sake,
who died for our sins and rose for our justification,
and now stands at your right hand to make intercession for us,
Jesus Christ our Lord.

Forgive our foolish ways

John Greenleaf Whittier

Dear Lord and Father of mankind,
  Forgive our foolish ways;
Reclothe us in our rightful mind,
In purer lives Thy service find,
  In deeper reverence, praise.

In simple trust like theirs who heard,
  Beside the Syrian sea,
The gracious calling of the Lord,
Let us, like them, without a word,
  Rise up and follow Thee.

O Sabbath rest by Galilee,
  O calm of hills above,
Where Jesus knelt to share with Thee
The silence of eternity,
  Interpreted by love!

With that deep hush subduing all
  Our words and works that drown
The tender whisper of Thy call,
As noiseless let Thy blessing fall
  As fell Thy manna down.

Drop Thy still dews of quietness,
  Till all our strivings cease;
Take from our souls the strain and stress,
And let our ordered lives confess
  The beauty of Thy peace.

Breathe through the heats of our desire
  Thy coolness and Thy balm;
Let sense be dumb, let flesh retire;
Speak through the earthquake, wind, and fire,
  O still, small voice of calm.

Conversion and Commitment
Amazing grace!

John Newton

Amazing grace! how sweet the sound
That saved a wretch like me;
I once was lost, but now am found;
Was blind, but now I see.

'Twas grace that taught my heart to fear,
And grace my fear relieved;
How precious did that grace appear,
The hour I first believed!

Through many dangers, toils and snares
I have already come:
'Tis grace that brought me safe thus far,
And grace will lead me home.

The Lord has promised good to me,
His word my hope secures;
He will my shield and portion be
As long as life endures.

Yes, when this heart and flesh shall fail,
And mortal life shall cease,
I shall profess within the veil
A life of joy and peace.

When we've been there a thousand years,
Bright shining as the sun,
We've no less days to sing God's praise
Than when we first begun.

Salvation is of Christ

St Patrick

I bind to myself the name,
the strong name of the Trinity;
by invocation of the same,
The Three in One, and One in Three.
Of whom all nature has creation;
eternal Father, Spirit, Word:
Praise to the Lord of my salvation,
Salvation is of Christ the Lord.

Love bade me welcome

George Herbert

Love bade me welcome: yet my soul drew back,
  Guilty of dust and sin.
But quick-ey'd Love, observing me grow slack
  From my first entrance in,
Drew nearer to me, sweetly questioning,
  If I lack'd any thing.

A guest, I answer'd, worthy to be here:
  Love said, You shall be he.
I the unkind, ungrateful? Ah my dear,
  I cannot look on thee.
Love took my hand, and smiling did reply,
  Who made the eyes but I?

Truth, Lord, but I have marr'd them: let my shame
  Go where it doth deserve.
And know you not, says Love, who bore the blame?
  My dear, then I will serve.
You must sit down, says Love, and taste my meat:
  So I did sit and eat.

Visit us with Thy salvation

Charles Wesley

Love divine, all loves excelling,
  Joy of heaven, to earth come down;
Fix in us thy humble dwelling;
All thy faithful mercies crown!
Jesus, Thou art all compassion,
Pure unbounded love Thou art;
Visit us with Thy salvation;
Enter every trembling heart.

Ravish me

John Donne

Batter my heart, three-person'd God, for you
As yet but knock, breathe, shine, and seek to mend.
That I may rise and stand, o'erthrow me, and bend
Your force to break, blow, burn, and make me new.
I, like an usurp'd town, to another due
Labour to admit you, but O, to no end!
Reason, your viceroy in me, me should defend,
But is captiv'd and proves weak or untrue.
Yet dearly I love you, and would be loved fain,
But am betrothed unto your enemy;
Divorce me, untie, or break that knot again,
Take me to you, imprison me, for I
Except you enthral me, never shall be free,
Nor ever chaste, except you ravish me.

To obtain for us everlasting life

Archbishop Robert Hamilton

Glory be to God in the highest,
Lord of heaven and earth,

who so loved the world
as to send his only Son
to redeem us from sin,
and to obtain for us everlasting life.
All praise be to you, most gracious God,
for your infinite mercies towards us in Jesus Christ our Lord.

You are the Way, the Truth, and the Life

Desiderius Erasmus
Glory be to God in the highest,
Help us not to stray from you, for you are the Way;
nor to distrust you, for you are the Truth;
nor to rest on any other than you, as you are the Life.
You have taught us what to believe, what to do, what to hope, and
    where to take our rest.
Give us grace to follow you, the Way, to learn from you, the Truth, and
    live in you, the Life.

Baptism
The significance of baptism

William Law, Christian Regeneration

Our baptism is to signify our seeking and obtaining a new birth.
And our being baptized in, or into the name of the Father, Son
and Holy Ghost, tells us in the plainest manner, what birth it is
that we seek, namely, such a new birth as may make us again what
we were at first, a living real image or offspring of the Father, Son,
and Holy Ghost.

It is owned on all hands, that we are baptized into a renovation
of some divine birth that we had lost; and that we may not be at
a loss to know what that divine birth is, the form in baptism
openly declares to us, that it is to regain that first birth of Father,
Son and Holy Ghost in our souls, which at the first made us to
be truly and really images of the nature of the Holy Trinity in

Unity. The form in baptism is but very imperfectly apprehended, till it is understood to have this great meaning in it. And it must be owned, that the scriptures tend wholly to guide us to this understanding of it. For since they teach us a birth of God, a birth of the Spirit, that we must obtain, and that baptism, the appointed sacrament of this new birth, is to be done in the name of the Father, Son, and Holy Ghost, can there be any doubt, that this sacrament is to signify the renovation of the birth of the Holy Trinity in our souls? ...

What an harmonious agreement does there thus appear, between our creation and redemption? and how finely, how surprisingly do our first and our second birth answer to, and illustrate one another?

Strengthen you with his grace

Martin Luther, blessing after a baptism

Almighty God, the Father of our Lord Jesus Christ, who has given you new birth through water and the Holy Spirit, and has forgiven you all your sin, strengthen you with his grace to life everlasting. Amen. Peace be with you.

Baptism and Conversion

Augustine, Sermons, on Psalm 103

Renewal does not happen in one moment of conversion, as the baptismal renewal by the forgiveness of all sins happens in a moment, so that not even one small sin remains unforgiven. But it is one thing to throw off a fever, another to recover from the weakness which the fever leaves behind it; it is one thing to remove from the body a missile stuck in it, another to heal the wound it made with a complete cure. The first stage of the cure is to remove the cause of the debility, and this is done by pardoning all sins; the second stage is curing the debility itself, and this is done gradually by making steady progress in the renewal of this image. These two stages are seen in Psalm 103:3, where we read, 'who forgives all your sins', which happens at baptism, 'and heals all your diseases', which happens by daily advances while the image is being renewed. The apostle Paul speaks about this quite clearly in 2 Corinthians 4:16: 'Though outwardly we are wasting away, yet inwardly we are being renewed day by day.'

Doubt
Many a doubt

Charlotte Elliott

Just as I am, without one plea
But that thy blood was shed for me,
And that thou bidd'st me come to thee,
O Lamb of God, I come.

Just as I am, though tossed about
With many a conflict, many a doubt,
Fightings within, and fears without,
O Lamb of God, I come.

Just as I am, poor, wretched, blind;
Sight, riches, healing of the mind,
Yea all I need, in thee to find,
O Lamb of God, I come.

Just as I am, thou wilt receive,
Wilt welcome, pardon, cleanse, relieve:
Because thy promise I believe,
O Lamb of God, I come.

Just as I am (thy love unknown
Has broken every barrier down),
Now to be thine, yea thine alone,
O Lamb of God, I come.

Just as I am, of that free love
The breadth, length, depth and height to prove,
Here for a season then above,
O Lamb of God, I come.

Embracings of love

Richard Baxter, The Saints' Everlasting Rest
Here is the heaven of heaven! This is the saint's fruition of God; it consists in these sweet, mutual, constant actions and embracings of love. To love, and to be loved: these are the everlasting arms that are underneath (Deuteronomy 33:27). His left hand is under their heads, and with his right hand doth he embrace them (Song of Songs 2:6).

Reader, stop here and think a moment what a state this is. Is it a small thing in your eyes to be loved by God – to be the son, the spouse, the love, the delight of the King of glory? Christian, believe this, and think about it: you will be eternally embraced in the arms of the love which was from everlasting, and will extend to everlasting – of the love which brought the Son of God's love from heaven to earth, from earth to the cross, from the cross to the grave, from the grave to glory – that love which was weary, hungry, tempted, scorned, scourged, buffeted, spat upon, crucified, pierced – which fasted, prayed, taught, healed, wept, sweated, bled, died. That love will eternally embrace you.

When perfect, created love and most perfect, uncreated love meet together, what a blessed meeting it will be!

Litany to the Holy Spirit

Robert Herrick
In the hour of my distress,
When temptations me oppress,
And when I my sins confess,
*   Sweet Spirit, comfort me!*

When I lie within my bed,
Sick in heart and sick in head,
And with doubts discomforted,
    Sweet Spirit, comfort me!

When the house doth sigh and weep,
And the world is drowned in sleep,
Yet mine eyes the watch do keep,
    Sweet Spirit, comfort me!

When the artless Doctor sees
No one hope but of his fees,
And his skill runs on the lees,
    Sweet Spirit, comfort me!

When the Tempter me pursu'th
With the sins of all my youth,
And half damns me with untruth,
    Sweet Spirit, comfort me!

When the passing bell doth toll,
And the furies in a shoal
Come to fright a parting soul,
    Sweet Spirit, comfort me!

When the tapers now burn blue,
And the comforters are few,
And that number more than true,
    Sweet Spirit, comfort me...

When, God knows, I'm tossed about,
Either with despair, or doubt;
Yet before the glass be out,
    Sweet Spirit, comfort me...

When the judgement is revealed,
And that opened which was sealed,
When to thee I have appealed,
　　Sweet Spirit comfort me!

Assurance
Daily increase

Gelasian Sacramentary
Come, Holy Spirit, and daily increase in these your servants your many gifts of grace: the spirit of wisdom and understanding, the spirit of counsel and strength, the spirit of knowledge and true godliness; and fill them with the spirit of your holy fear, now and evermore.

Establish and confirm

Clement of Rome
Almighty God, Father of our Lord Jesus Christ, establish and confirm us in your truth by your Holy Spirit. Reveal to us what we do not know; perfect in us what is lacking; strengthen us in what we know; and keep us faultless in your service; through the same Jesus Christ our Lord.

O Jesus, I have promised

John Ernest Bode
O Jesus, I have promised
To serve thee to the end;
Be thou for ever near me,
My Master and my Friend!
I shall not fear the battle
If thou art by my side,
Nor wander from the pathway
If thou wilt be my Guide.

O let me hear thee speaking
In accents clear and still,
Above the storms of passion,
The murmurs of self-will.
O speak to reassure me,
To hasten or control;
O speak, and make me listen,
Thou guardian of my soul.

O Jesus, thou hast promised
To all who follow thee,
That where thou art in glory
There shall thy servant be;
And, Jesus, I have promised
To serve thee to the end;
O give me grace to follow,
My Master and my Friend.

O let me see thy footmarks,
And in them plant mine own:
My hope to follow duly
Is in thy strength alone.
O guide me, call me, draw me,
Uphold me to the end;
And then in heaven receive me,
My Saviour and my Friend!

It's done: the great transaction's done!

Philip Doddridge

O happy day, that fixed my choice
On Thee, my Saviour and my God!
Well may this glowing heart rejoice,
And tell its raptures all abroad.

Refrain

O happy day, O happy day, when Jesus washed my sins away!
He taught me how to watch and pray, and live rejoicing every day
O happy day, O happy day, when Jesus washed my sins away.

It's done: the great transaction's done!
O happy bond, that seals my vows
To Him Who merits all my love!
Let cheerful anthems fill His house,
While to that sacred shrine I move.

Refrain

It's done: the great transaction's done!
I am the Lord's and He is mine;
He drew me and I followed on;
Charmed to confess the voice divine.

Refrain

Now rest, my long divided heart,
Fixed on this blissful centre, rest.
Here have I found a nobler part;
Here heavenly pleasures fill my breast.

Refrain

High heaven, that heard the solemn vow,
That vow renewed shall daily hear,
Till in life's latest hour I bow
And bless in death a bond so dear.

Refrain

Bring me home to your fold again

Jerome

O good Shepherd, seek me, and bring me home to your fold again. I am like the man on the road to Jericho who was attacked by robbers, wounded and left half dead. You who are the Good Samaritan, lift me up, and deal favourably with me according to your good pleasure, until I may dwell in your house all the days of my life, and praise you for ever and ever with those who are there.

Dedication
Consecration

Frances Ridley Havergal

Take my life, and let it be
Consecrated, Lord, to thee;
Take my moments and my days,
Let them flow in ceaseless praise.

That I may live only for thee

Gertrude of Thüringen

O Love, O God, you created me, in your love recreate me.

O Love, you redeemed me, fill up and redeem for yourself in me whatever part of your love has fallen into neglect within me.

O Love, O God, you made me yours, as in the blood of your Christ you purchased me, in your truth sanctify me.

O Love, O God, you adopted me as a daughter, after your own heart fashion and foster me.

O Love, you chose me as yours not another's, grant that I may cling to you with my whole being.

O Love, O God, you loved me first, grant that with my whole heart, and with my whole soul, and with my whole strength, I may love you.

O Love, O God almighty, in your love confirm me.

O Love most wise, give me wisdom in the love of you.

O Love most sweet, give me sweetness in the taste of you.

O Love most dear, grant that I may live only for you.

O Love most faithful, in all my tribulations comfort and succour me.

O Love who is always with me, work all my works in me.

O Love most victorious, grant that I may persevere to the end in you.

Working in the light of heaven

Henry Martyn

Send out your light and your truth, that I may live always near to you, my God. Let me feel your love, that I may be as it were already in heaven, that I may do my work as the angels do theirs; and let me be ready for every work, ready to go out or go in, to stay or depart, just as you direct.

Lord, let me have no will of my own, or consider my true happiness as depending in the smallest degree on anything that happens to me outwardly, but as consisting totally in conformity to your will.

I am all yours and all in you

Francis de Sales

Lord, I am yours,
and I must belong to no one but you.
My soul is yours,
and must live only through you.
My will is yours,
and must love only for you.
I must love you as my first cause,
since I am from you.
I must love you as my goal and rest,
since I am for you.

I must love you more than my own being,
since my being comes from you.
I must love you more than myself,
since I am all yours and all in you. Amen.

Lord, I believe in you

The Universal Prayer, *attributed to Pope Clement XI*

Lord, I believe in you – increase my faith.

I trust in you – strengthen my trust.

I love you – let me love you more and more.

I am sorry for my sins – deepen my sorrow.

I worship you as my first beginning, I long for you as my last end, I praise you as my constant helper, and call on you as my loving protector.

Guide me by your wisdom, correct me with your justice, comfort me with your mercy, protect me with your power.

I offer you, Lord, my thoughts – to be fixed on you; my words – to have you for their theme; my actions – to reflect my love for you; my sufferings – to be endured for your greater glory.

I want to do what you ask of me – in the way you ask, for as long as you ask, because you ask it.

Lord, enlighten my understanding, strengthen my will, purify my heart, and make me holy.

Help me to repent of my past sins and to resist temptation in the future. Help me to rise above my human weaknesses and to grow stronger as a Christian.

Let me love you, my Lord and my God, and see myself as I really am – a pilgrim in this world, a Christian called to respect and to love all whose lives I touch, those in authority over me or those under my authority, my friends and my enemies.

Help me to conquer anger with gentleness, greed with generosity, apathy by fervour. Help me to forget myself and reach out to others.

Make me prudent in planning, courageous in taking risks. Make me patient in suffering, unassuming in prosperity.

Keep me, Lord, attentive at prayer, temperate in food and drink, diligent in my work, firm in my good intentions.

Let my conscience be clear, my conduct without fault, my speech blameless, and my life well-ordered.

Teach me to realize that this world is passing, that my true future is the happiness of heaven, that life on earth is short, and the life to come eternal.

Help me prepare for death with a proper fear of judgement, and a greater trust in your goodness.

Lead me safely through death to the endless joy of heaven.

Grant this through Christ our Lord. Amen

Forgiveness

Prayer on a plaque on the altar of Coventry Cathedral, written in 1964

The hatred which divides nation from nation,
race from race, class from class,
Father, forgive.

The covetous desires of men and nations
to possess what is not their own,
Father, forgive.

The greed which exploits the labours of men,
and lays waste the earth,
Father, forgive.

Our envy of the welfare and happiness of others,
Father, forgive.

Our indifference to the plight of the homeless and the refugee,
Father, forgive.

The lust which uses for ignoble ends
the bodies of men and women,
Father, forgive.

The pride which leads to trust in ourselves
and not in God,
Father, forgive.

Love, power, grace

Gallican Sacramentary
Grant to your servants, O God,
to be set on fire with your love,
to be strengthened by your power,
to be illuminated by your Spirit,
to be filled with your grace,
and to go forward by your help;
through Jesus Christ our Lord.

Wills to obey

Christina Rossetti
Speak, Lord, for Thy servant heareth.
Grant us ears to hear,
eyes to see,
wills to obey,
hearts to love;
then declare what Thou wilt,
reveal what Thou wilt,
command what Thou wilt,
demand what Thou wilt.

Let us possess ourselves in patience

Jeremy Taylor

Take from us, O God, all tediousness of spirit, all impatience and unquietness. Let us possess ourselves in patience, through Jesus Christ our Lord.

Pride and self-assertion

Leonine Sacramentary

O God, who resists the proud, and gives grace to the humble: grant us the virtue of true humility, which your only-begotten Son himself gave us the perfect example; that we may never offend you by our pride, and be rejected by our self-assertion; through Jesus Christ our Lord.

To think humbly on ourselves

Jane Austen

Incline us, O God, to think humbly on ourselves, to be saved only in the examination of our own conduct, to consider our fellow creatures with kindness, and to judge of all they say and do with the charity which we would desire from them ourselves.

Surrender

Ignatius Loyola

Take, Lord, and receive all my liberty,
my memory, my understanding,
and my whole will.
All that I have and call my own,
you have given to me.
I surrender it all to you
to be disposed of according to your will.

Give me only your love and your grace;
with these I will be rich enough,
and will desire nothing more.

True humility

John Cosin

Give us true humility, a meek and a quiet spirit, a loving and a
friendly, a holy and a useful conversation, bearing the burdens of
our neighbours, denying ourselves, and studying to benefit others,
and to please thee in all things.

Obedience

Lancelot Andrewes

Open my eyes that I may see,
Incline my heart that I may desire,
Order my steps that I may follow
The way of Thy commandments.

I give thee my body, my soul

John Cosin

Be thou a light to my eyes, music to my ears, sweetness to my
taste, and full contentment to my heart. Be thou my sunshine
in the day, my food at table, my repose in the night, my clothing
in nakedness, and my succour in all necessities. Lord Jesu, I give
thee my body, my soul, my substance, my fame, my friends, my
liberty and my life. Dispose of me and all that is mine as it may
seem best to thee and to the glory of thy blessed name.

Patient persevering obedience

Richard Baxter
Let the eternal God be the portion of my soul;
let heaven be my inheritance and hope;
let Christ be my Head, and my promise of security;
let faith be my wisdom,
and love my very heart and will,
and patient persevering obedience be my life;
and then I can spare the wisdom of the world,
because I can spare the trifles that it seeks,
and all that they are like to get by it.

Patience

George Herbert, The Temple
The church floor
Mark you the floor? That square and speckled stone,
Which looks so firm and strong,
Is Patience:
And th' other black and grave, wherewith each one
Is chequer'd all along,
Humility:
The gentle rising, which on either hand
Leads to the quire above,
Is Confidence:
But the sweet cement, which in one sure band
Ties the whole frame, is Love
And Charity.

Deliver us from evil

Alcuin

Eternal Light, shine into our hearts,
    eternal Goodness, deliver us from evil,
    eternal Power, be our support,
    eternal Wisdom, scatter the darkness of our ignorance,
    eternal Pity, have mercy upon us;
    that with all our heart and mind and strength we may seek thy
face and be brought by your infinite mercy to your holy presence; through Jesus Christ our Lord.

Perseverance

Source unknown, based on a saying of Sir Francis Drake

O Lord God, when Thou givest to Thy servants to endeavour any great matter, grant us also to know that it is not the beginning, but the continuing of the same to the end, until it be thoroughly finished, which yieldeth the true glory; through Him who for the finishing of Thy work laid down his life, our Redeemer, Jesus Christ.

To be a pilgrim

John Bunyan

Who would true valour see,
Let him come hither;
One here will constant be,
Come wind, come weather.
There's no discouragement
Shall make him once relent
His first avow'd intent
To be a pilgrim.

The way of peace

Sarum Missal
O Lord, look mercifully on us, and grant that we may always choose the way of peace.

The Pilgrimage

Sir Walter Raleigh, written when he was a prisoner in the Tower of London, awaiting execution
The scallop-shell was a symbol of pilgrimage in the Middle Ages.

Give me my scallop-shell of quiet,
My staff of faith to walk upon,
My scrip of joy, immortal diet,
My bottle of salvation,
My gown of glory, hope's true gage;
And thus I'll take my pilgrimage.

Blood must be my body's balmer;
No other balm will there be given;
Whilst my soul, like quiet palmer,
Travelleth towards the land of heaven;
Over the silver mountains,
Where spring the nectar fountains:
There will I kiss
The bowl of bliss,
And drink mine everlasting fill
Upon every milken hill.
My soul will be a-dry before;
But, after, it will thirst no more...

From thence to heaven's Bribeless hall
Where no corrupted voices brawl,
No Conscience molten into gold,
Nor forged accusers bought and sold,

No cause deferred, nor vain spent journey,
For there Christ is the King's Attorney:
Who pleads for all without degrees,
And he hath Angels, but no fees.

When the grand twelve million Jury,
Of our sins with dreadful fury,
'Gainst our souls black verdicts give,
Christ pleads his death, and then we live,
Be thou my speaker, taintless pleader,
Unblotted Lawyer, true proceeder,
Thou movest salvation even for alms:
Not with a bribed Lawyer's palms.

And this is my eternal plea,
To him that made Heaven, Earth and Sea,
Seeing my flesh must die so soon,
And want a head to dine next noon,
Just at the stroke when my veins start and spread
Set on my soul an everlasting head.
Then am I ready like a palmer fit,
To tread those blest paths which before I writ.

Lukewarmness

John Wesley

Deliver me, Lord God, from a slothful mind, from all lukewarmness, and all dejection of spirit. I know these cannot but deaden my love for you; mercifully free my heart from them, and give me a lively, zealous, active and cheerful spirit; that I may vigorously perform whatever you command, thankfully suffer whatever you choose for me, and always be ardent to obey in all things your holy love.

I give you my hands

Lancelot Andrewes
Lord Jesus,
    I give you my hands to do your work,
    I give you my feet to go your way,
    I give you my eyes to see as you do.
    I give you my tongue to speak your words,
    I give you my mind that you may think in me,
    I give you my spirit that you may pray in me.
    Above all, I give you my heart that you may love in me, your Father, and all mankind.
    I give you my whole self that you may grow in me, so that it is you, Lord Jesus, who live and work and pray in me.
    I hand over to your care, Lord, my soul and body, my mind and thoughts, my prayers and hopes, my health and work, my life and my death, my parents and my family, my friends and my neighbours, my country and all men. Today and always.

Self-control

B.F. Westcott
Almighty and everlasting God, who for the well-being of our earthly life has put into our hearts wholesome desires of body and spirit: Mercifully increase and establish in us, we beseech you, the grace of holy discipline and healthy self-control; that we may fulfil our desires by the means which you have given, and for the ends you have ordained; through Jesus Christ our Lord.

Dedication

Dr Johnson
Almighty God, in whose hands are all the powers of men, grant that we may not lavish away the life which you have given us on useless trifles; but enable us by your Holy Spirit so to shun sloth

and negligence that every day we may carry out the task which you have allotted us, and obtain such success as will most promote your glory; for the sake of Jesus Christ.

An unconquered heart

Thomas Aquinas

Give us, O Lord, a steadfast heart, which no unworthy affection may drag downwards; an unconquered heart, which no tribulation can wear out; give us an upright heart, which no unworthy purpose may tempt aside. Bestow on us also, O Lord, understanding to know you, diligence to seek you, wisdom to find you and a faithfulness that may finally embrace you; through Jesus Christ our Lord.

So shall my walk be close with God

William Cowper

O for a closer walk with God,
*   A calm and heavenly frame;*
A light to shine upon the road
*   That leads me to the Lamb!*

Return, O holy Dove, return,
*   Sweet messenger of rest;*
I hate the sins that made thee mourn,
*   And drove thee from my breast.*

The dearest idol I have known,
*   Whate'er that idol be,*
Help me to tear it from thy throne,
*   And worship only thee.*

So shall my walk be close with God,
  Calm and serene my frame;
So purer light shall mark the road
  That leads me to the Lamb.

Jesus, my life

John Newton

If ask'd, what of Jesus I think?
Though still my best thoughts are but poor,
I say, He's my meat and my drink,
My life, and my strength, and my store;
My shepherd, my husband, my friend,
My Saviour from sin and from thrall;
My hope from beginning to end,
My portion, my Lord, and my all.

Keep my tongue from evil

The Treasury of Devotion

Set a watch, O Lord, before my mouth, and keep the door of my lips.
Lord, keep my tongue from evil, and my lips that they speak no guile.

Take me from myself

Nicholas of Flue

My Lord and my God, take me from all that keeps me from you.
My Lord and my God, grant me all that leads me to you.
My Lord and my God, take me from myself and give me completely to you.

Holy Communion
Everlasting fellowship

B.F. Westcott

Almighty God, who has given your only Son to die for us: Grant that we who have been united in the communion of his most precious Body and Blood may be so cleansed from our past sins, and so strengthened to follow the example of his most holy life, that we may hereafter enjoy everlasting fellowship with you in heaven, through him who loved us and gave himself for us, the same Jesus Christ our Lord.

Living food

Thomas Cranmer, Defence of the True and Catholic Doctrine of the Sacrament

Our Saviour Christ is both the first beginner of our spiritual life (who first begetteth us into God his Father), and also afterwards he is our lively food and spiritual life.

What the word did make it, I believe

Elizabeth I, in answer to a question concerning her belief about the presence of Christ in the bread and wine

'Twas God the word that spake it,
He took the bread and brake it;
And what the word did make it,
That I believe, and take it.

Commemoration and unity

Author unknown, The Companion or Spiritual Guide at the Altar, 1783

After the *bread* and *wine* are deputed by holy prayer to God, to be used for a commemoration of Christ's death, though they do not cease to be what they were before; yet, they become something, which they were not before consecration: They become visible signs or pledges of that inward and spiritual grace, which they are appointed by Christ himself, to represent; which grace is no less than the *body and blood of Christ, which are verily and indeed taken and received by the faithful in the Lord's Supper.* For they have a real feel and portion given them in the death and sufferings of the Lord Jesus; whose body was broken and blood shed for the remission of sins. They truly and indeed partake of the virtue of his bloody sacrifice, whereby he hath obtained an eternal redemption for mankind. And it is the nature and office of these sacramental pledges to assure us of the good will of God, and of his truth in fulfilling his gracious promises. He engages to be faithful to us in 'giving' them, as we engage ourselves to be faithful to him in 'receiving' them.

...This sacrament is also a bond of union amongst Christians. They, who believe in one common Saviour, and partake of the same sacrifice, will never forget the duty of that lesson. *Beloved, if God so loved us,* as to give his only begotten Son, to die for our sins, *we ought also to love one another.* The sacrifice here offered is declarative of Christian unanimity, knit together in a firm and inseparable charity.

I will receive forgiveness

Martin Luther

Lord, I am indeed unworthy that you should come under my roof, but I need and long for your help and grace that I may walk in the right path. Therefore, I come to you, trusting only in the comforting words which I have heard, which you invite me with

to your table and say to me, who is so unworthy, that I will receive
forgiveness of my sins through your body and blood, if I eat and
drink of this sacrament. Amen! Dear Lord, I do not doubt that
your Word is true, and relying on this promise I eat and drink
with you. Let it happen to me according to your will and Word.

Welcome

William Cowper
Welcome to the Table
This is the feast of heav'nly wine,
And God invites to sup;
The juices of the living vine
Were pressed, to fill the cup.

O, bless the Saviour, ye that eat,
With royal dainties fed;
Not heav'n affords a costlier treat,
For Jesus is the bread!

The vile, the lost, he calls to them,
Ye trembling souls appear!
The righteous, in their own esteem,
Have no acceptance here.

Approach, ye poor, nor dare refuse
The banquet spread for you;
Dear Saviour, this is welcome news,
That I may venture too.

If guilt and sin afford a plea,
And may obtain a place;
Surely the Lord will welcome me,
And I shall see his face!

Face to face

Horatius Bonar

Here, O my Lord, I see thee face to face;
Here would I touch and handle things unseen,
Here grasp with firmer hand the eternal grace,
And all my weariness upon thee lean.

Here would I feed upon the bread of God,
Here drink with thee the royal wine of heaven;
Here would I lay aside each earthly load,
Here taste afresh the calm of sin forgiven.

Mine is the sin, but thine the righteousness;
Mine is the guilt, but thine the cleansing blood;
Here is my robe, my refuge, and my peace –
Thy blood, thy righteousness, O Lord, my God.

This salutary gift

Martin Luther

We give thanks to you, almighty God, that you have refreshed us with this salutary gift; and we pray that in your mercy you will strengthen our faith in you, and in fervent love towards one another; through Jesus Christ, your dear Son, our Lord, who lives and reigns with you and the Holy Spirit, ever one God, world without end.

Before Holy Communion

Thomas Aquinas

Almighty, everlasting God, I draw near to the sacrament of your only-begotten Son, our Lord Jesus Christ.

I who am sick approach the physician of life.

I who am unclean come to the fountain of mercy;

blind, to the light of eternal brightness;
poor and needy, to the Lord of heaven and earth.
Therefore, I pray that you will, in your endless mercy,
heal my sickness, cleanse my defilement,
enlighten my blindness, enrich my poverty,
and clothe my nakedness.
Then shall I dare to receive the bread of angels,
the King of kings and Lord of lords,
with reverence and humility, contrition and love,
purity and faith, with the purpose and intention necessary for
the good of my soul.

The food of everlasting life

John Calvin

We offer you immortal praise and thanks, heavenly Father, for the great blessing which you have conferred on us miserable sinners, in allowing us to partake of your Son Jesus Christ, whom was handed over to die for us, and now gives us the food of everlasting life. So we dedicate the rest of our lives to advance your glory and build up our neighbours, through the same Jesus Christ your Son, who, in the unity of the Holy Spirit, lives with you and reigns for ever.

Preparing for the Lord's Supper

Thomas Ken

Glory be to Thee, O Lord, who makest Thine own Body and Blood to become our spiritual food, to strengthen and refresh our souls.

Glory be to Thee, O Lord, who by this heavenly food dost mystically unite us to Thyself; for nothing becomes one with our bodies more than the bodily food we eat, which turns into our very substance, and nothing makes us to become one with Thee more, than when Thou vouchsafest to become the very food of our souls!

Glory be to Thee, O Lord, who by this immortal food dost nourish our souls to live the life of grace here, and dost raise us up to life everlasting hereafter! Lord, do Thou evermore give us this bread! Amen, Amen.

Growth in Holiness
This ravishing

Richard Rolle, The Fire of Love

The closer and more present God is to a soul, the purer is his love. This is how one rejoices more purely in God. He feels more strongly God's goodness and loving-kindness which is bound to be poured out in those who love him. With incomparable joy it fills to overflowing the hearts of the just.

With great purity the spirit is totally established in a single desire for eternity, and looks up continually, with freedom, towards heavenly things. It is so caught up that it is ravished from every other thing to which it does not turn and cannot love.

But this ravishing, however, is clearly to be understood in two ways. In one way, he is so ravished out of bodily feeling that at the time of rapture he cannot feel whatever is done in or from the flesh. He is not, however, dead, but alive, because the soul yet quickens the body. In this way the saints and the elect are some-times enraptured for the benefit and instruction of others, as Paul was ravished in the third heaven. In this way too sinners are sometimes ravished so that they may see the joy of the blessed or the punishments of the damned, in order that they themselves or others may be corrected. And we read of many such examples.

In the other way, it is called the rapture of the raising of the mind to God by contemplation. This is found in all the perfect lovers of God, and in no one unless they love God. It is correctly called rapture or ravishing, like the other, because it does a certain violence, as it were, against nature. Moreover, it is truly supernatural, since it may change a man from a vile sinner to a son of God, who is carried up into God, full of spiritual joy.

Let grace work

George Herbert, The Temple

My stock lies dead, and no increase
Doth my dull husbandry improve:
O let thy graces without cease
Drop from above!
If still the Sun should hide his face,
Thy house would but a dungeon prove,
Thy works night's captives: O let grace
Drop from above!
The dew doth every morning fall;
And shall the dew outstrip thy Dove?
The dew, for which grass cannot call,
Drop from above!
Death is still working like a mole,
And digs my grave at each remove:
Let grace work too, and on my soul
Drop from above!
Sin is still hammering my heart
Unto a hardness, void of love:
Let suppling grace, to cross his art,
Drop from above!
O come! for thou dost know the way.
Or if to me thou wilt not move,
Remove me where I need not say –
Drop from above!

I asked God for strength ... I was made weak

'A Soldier's Prayer', written by an anonymous confederate soldier in the American civil war

I asked God for strength, that I might achieve,
I was made weak, that I might learn humbly to obey.
I asked for health, that I might do greater things,
I was given infirmity, that I might do better things.

I asked for riches, that I might be happy,
I was given poverty, that I might be wise.
I asked for power, that I might have the praise of men,
I was given weakness, that I might feel the need of God.
I asked for all things, that I might enjoy life,
I was given life, that I might enjoy all things.
I got nothing that I asked for –
but everything that I had hoped for,
almost despite myself, my unspoken prayers were answered.
I am among all men most richly blessed.

Grant that I may perceive my own transgressions

Ephraem
O Lord and Master of my life,
Grant that I may not have a spirit of idleness,
of discouragement,
of lust for power,
and of vain speaking.
But bestow on me, your servant,
the spirit of chastity,
of meekness,
of patience,
and of love.
Yes, O Lord and King,
grant that I may perceive
my own transgressions,
and judge not my brother,
For you are blessed from age to age.

Temptations
Troubles and temptations

Augustine

O God, by thy mercy strengthen us who lie exposed to the rough storms of troubles and temptations. Help us against our own negligence and cowardice, and defend us from the treachery of our unfaithful hearts. Succour us, we beseech thee, and bring us to thy safe haven of peace and felicity.

O Lord seek us, O Lord find us

Christina Rossetti

O Lord seek us, O Lord find us
In Thy patient care,
Be Thy love before, behind us,
Round us everywhere.
Lest the god of this world blind us,
Lest he bait a snare,
Lest he forge a chain to bind us,
Lest he speak us fair,
Turn not from us, call to mind us,
Find, embrace us, hear.
By Thy love before, behind us,
Round us everywhere.

Against the temptations of the world

The breastplate of St Patrick

I rise today with the power of God to guide me,
the might of God to uphold me,
the wisdom of God to teach me,
the eye of God to watch over me,
the ear of God to hear me,
the word of God to give me speech,

the hand of God to protect me,
the path of God to lie before me,
the shield of God to shelter me,
the host of God to defend me
against the snares of the devil and the temptations of the world,
against every man who meditates injury to me,
whether far or near.

Nail down our flesh with fear of Thee

Basil the Great

O God and Lord of the Powers, and Maker of all creation, who, because of Your clemency and incomparable mercy, didst send Thine Only-Begotten Son and our Lord Jesus Christ for the salvation of mankind, and with His venerable cross didst tear asunder the record of our sins, and thereby didst conquer the rulers and powers of darkness; receive from us sinful people, O merciful Master, these prayers of gratitude and supplication, and deliver us from every destructive and gloomy transgression, and from all visible and invisible enemies who seek to injure us. Nail down our flesh with fear of Thee, and let not our hearts be inclined to words or thoughts of evil, but pierce our souls with Your love, that ever contemplating Thee, being enlightened by Thee, and discerning Thee, the unapproachable and everlasting Light, we may unceasingly render confession and gratitude to Thee: The eternal Father, with Thine Only-Begotten Son, and with Thine All-Holy, Gracious, and Life-Giving Spirit, now and ever, and unto ages of ages. Amen.

Battling against evil

The Treasury of Devotion

Help me now, O God, to do all things in your sight, who sees in secret.

Shut out, O God, from my heart everything that offends you.

By your mighty power, repress all my wandering thoughts, and tread down Satan under my feet.

While the tempest still is high

Charles Wesley

Jesu, lover of my soul,
   let me to Thy bosom fly,
While the nearer waters roll,
   while the tempest still is high.
Hide me, O my Saviour, hide,
   till the storm of life is past;
Safe into the haven guide;
   O receive my soul at last.

Other refuge have I none,
   hangs my helpless soul on Thee;
Leave, ah! leave me not alone,
   still support and comfort me.
All my trust on Thee is stayed,
   all my help from Thee I bring;
Cover my defenceless head
   with the shadow of Thy wing.

Wilt Thou not regard my call?
   Wilt Thou not accept my prayer?
Lo! I sink, I faint, I fall –
   Lo! on Thee I cast my care;
Reach me out Thy gracious hand!
   While I of Thy strength receive,
Hoping against hope I stand,
   dying, and behold, I live.

Thou, O Christ, art all I want,
   more than all in Thee I find;

Raise the fallen, cheer the faint,
  heal the sick, and lead the blind.
Just and holy is Thy Name,
  I am all unrighteousness;
False and full of sin I am;
  Thou art full of truth and grace.

Plenteous grace with Thee is found,
  grace to cover all my sin;
Let the healing streams abound;
  make and keep me pure within.
Thou of life the fountain art,
  freely let me take of Thee;
Spring Thou up within my heart;
  rise to all eternity.

Constancy in temptations

John Cosin

O Lord our God, grant us, we beseech thee, patience in troubles, humility in comforts, constancy in temptations, and victory over all our spiritual enemies. Grant us sorrow for our sins, thankfulness for your benefits, fear of your judgement, love of your mercies, and mindfulness of your presence; now and for evermore.

Abate our temptations

Christina Rossetti

Holy Spirit,
as the wind is thy symbol, so forward our goings,
as the dove, so launch us heavenwards,
as water, so purify our spirits,
as a cloud, so abate our temptations,
as dew, so revive our languor,
as fire, so purge out our dross.

Support us in time of temptation

B.F. Westcott

Blessed Lord, who was tempted in all things just as we are, have mercy on our frailty. Out of weakness give us strength. Grant us to reverence you, so that we may reverence you only. Support us in time of temptation. Make us bold in time of danger. Help us to do your work with courage, and to continue your faithful soldiers and servants to our life's end; through Jesus Christ our Lord.

Spiritual Dryness and Trials
My spirit is dry

John of the Cross

My spirit is dry within me because it forgets to feed on you.

An empty vessel that needs to be filled

Martin Luther

Behold, Lord, an empty vessel that needs to be filled. My Lord, fill it. I am weak in the faith; strengthen me. I am cold in love; warm me and make me fervent that my love may go out to my neighbour. O Lord, help me. Strengthen my faith and trust in you.

With me, there is an abundance of sin; in you is the fullness of righteousness. Therefore I will remain with you, from whom I can receive, but to whom I may not give.

He made me feel the hidden evils of my heart

John Newton

I asked the Lord, that I might grow
In faith, and love, and every grace;
Might more of His salvation know,
And seek more earnestly His face.

I hoped that in some favoured hour
At once He'd answer my request,
And by His love's constraining power
Subdue my sins, and give me rest.

Instead of this, He made me feel
The hidden evils of my heart;
And let the angry powers of hell
Assault my soul in every part.

Yea more, with His own hand He seemed
Intent to aggravate my woe;
Crossed all the fair designs I schemed,
Blasted my gourds, and laid me low.

'Lord, why is this?' I trembling cried,
'Wilt thou pursue Thy worm to death?'
''Tis in this way,' the Lord replied,
'I answer prayer for grace and faith.

'These inward trials I employ
From self and pride to set thee free;
And break thy schemes of earthly joy,
That thou may'st seek thy all in me.'

Renewal
Fill me with life anew

Edwin Hatch
Breathe on me, Breath of God;
Fill me with life anew,
That I may love what thou dost love,
And do what thou wouldst do.

Breathe on me, Breath of God,
Till I am wholly thine,
Until this earthly part of me
Glows with thy fire divine.

Breathe on me, Breath of God,
So shall I never die,
But live with thee the perfect life
Of thine eternity.

Stir up thy gift in me

Charles Wesley
O thou who camest from above,
The pure celestial fire to impart,
Kindle a flame of sacred love
On the mean altar of my heart.

There let it for thy glory burn,
With inextinguishable blaze;
And trembling to its source return,
In humble love and fervent praise.

Jesus, confirm my heart's desire
To work, and speak, and thank for thee;
Still let me guard the holy fire,
And still stir up thy gift in me.

Ready for all thy perfect will,
My acts of faith and love repeat,
Till death thy endless mercies seal,
And make the sacrifice complete.

Change us by the work of your Holy Spirit

Søren Kierkegaard
Our Father, you called us and saved us in order to make us like your Son, our Lord Jesus Christ. Day by day, change us by the work of your Holy Spirit so that we may grow more like him in all that we think and say and do, to his glory.

Come Holy Spirit, and inflame our hearts with your love

Francis de Sales, the concluding prayer in his book Treatise on the Love of God
O love eternal,
my soul needs and chooses you eternally.
O, come Holy Spirit,
and inflame our hearts with your love.
To love – or to die.
To die – and to love.
To die to all other love
in order to live in Jesus' love,
so that we may not die eternally.
But that we may live in your eternal love,
O Saviour of our souls,
we eternally sing,
'Live, Jesus.
Jesus, I love.
Live, Jesus, whom I love.
Jesus, I love,
Jesus who lives and reigns for ever and ever. Amen.'

The gentle movement of the Holy Spirit

Author unknown, Frankfurt prayer, sixteenth century
O Lord, the Scripture says, 'There is a time for silence and a time for speech.'

Saviour, teach me the silence of humility,
the silence of wisdom,
the silence of love,
the silence of perfection,
the silence that speaks without words,
the silence of faith.

Lord, teach me to silence my own heart that I may listen to the gentle movement of the Holy Spirit within me and be aware of your depths.

Take full possession of my heart

John Wesley

O Lord, take full possession of my heart, raise there your throne, and command there as you do in heaven.

Being created by you, let me live for you;
being created for you, let me always act for your glory;
being redeemed by you, let me give to you what is yours;
and let my spirit cling to you alone, for your name's sake.

Breathe in me

Augustine

Breathe in me, O Holy Spirit, that my thoughts may all be holy. Act in me, O Holy Spirit, that my work, too, may be holy. Draw my heart, O Holy Spirit, that I love but what is holy. Strengthen me, O Holy Spirit, to defend all that is holy. Guard me, then, O Holy Spirit, that I always may be holy.

Worship
Our full homage

Liturgy of St James
Let all mortal flesh keep silent, and with fear and trembling stand;
Ponder nothing earthly-minded, for with blessing in his hand,
Christ our God to earth descendeth, our full homage to command.

Father and Mother

Julian of Norwich, Revelations of Divine Love
God is as truly our Mother as he is our Father.

Our great Father, almighty God, who is being, knew and loved us before time began. In that knowledge, out of his wonderful deep love, and with the foresight and counsel of the blessed Trinity, he willed that the second person become our Mother.

Our Father willed it, our Mother accomplished it, our good Lord the Holy Spirit established it. So we must love our God in whom we have our being. We must reverently thank and praise him for our creation, fervently ask our Mother for mercy and compassion, and our Lord the Holy Spirit for help and grace.

From nature, mercy and grace – from these three – comes our life. From them we have humility and gentleness and pity. From them, too, we get our hatred of sin and wickedness, for it is in the nature of virtue to hate these.

So Jesus is our true Mother in nature because of our first creation, and he is our true Mother in grace because he took our created nature. In the second person there is all the loving service and sweet spontaneous care that belongs to beloved motherhood, and in him our will for God is always safe, both naturally and by grace, because of his own innate goodness.

I saw that the motherhood of God can be looked at in three ways. The first is his creation of our human nature; the second his assumption of nature – from which stems the motherhood of grace; and the third is the practical outworking of motherhood,

as a result of which, and by that same grace, it spreads out in endless height, breadth, length, and depth. And all is one here.

Praise, my soul, the King of heaven

H.F. Lyte, based on Psalm 103
Praise, my soul, the King of heaven;
To his feet thy tribute bring;
Ransomed, healed, restored, forgiven,
Who like thee his praise should sing?
Praise him, praise him,
Praise the everlasting King.

Praise him for his grace and favour
To our fathers in distress;
Praise him still the same for ever,
Slow to chide, and swift to bless:
Praise him, praise him,
Glorious in his faithfulness.

Father-like he tends and spares us;
Well our feeble frame he knows;
In his hands he gently bears us,
Rescues us from all our foes:
Praise him, praise him,
Widely as his mercy flows.

Angels, help us to adore him,
Ye behold him face to face;
Sun and moon, bow down before him;
Dwellers all in time and space,
Praise him, praise him.
Praise with us the God of grace.

I will praise thee

George Herbert, The Temple

King of glory, King of peace,
I will love thee:
And that love may never cease,
I will move thee.

Thou hast granted my request,
Thou has heard me:
Thou didst note my working breast,
Thou has spared me.

Wherefore with my utmost art
I will sing thee,
And the cream of all my heart
I will bring thee.

Though my sins against me cried,
Thou didst clear me;
And alone, when they replied,
Thou didst hear me.

Seven whole days, not one in seven,
I will praise thee.
In my heart, though not in heaven,
I can raise thee.

Thou grew'st soft and moist with tears,
Thou relentedst.
And when Justice call'd for fears,
Thou dissentedst.

Small it is, in this poor sort
To enrol thee:
Even eternity's too short
To extol thee.

The Body of Christ
The worldwide Church

William Laud
Gracious Father, I humbly beseech Thee for Thy Holy Catholic Church. Fill it with all truth, in all truth, with all peace. Where it is corrupt, purge it. Where it is in error, direct it. Where it is superstitious, rectify it. Where anything is amiss, reform it. Where it is right, strengthen and confirm it. Where it is in want, furnish it. Where it is divided and rent asunder, make up the breaches of it, O Thou Holy One of Israel.

Bring us to unity of love

Liturgy of St Dionysius
O God of peace, good beyond all that is good, in whom is calmness and concord: Heal the dissensions which divide us from one another, and bring us to unity of love in you; through Jesus Christ our Lord.

In unity of spirit

English reformers, 1549
O almighty God, who has built your church on the foundations of the apostles and prophets, Jesus Christ himself being the head cornerstone: grant us to be so joined together in unity of spirit by their teaching that we may be made into a holy temple, acceptable to you, through Jesus Christ our Lord.

Daily Prayers
I give you this day

Francis de Sales

My God, I give you this day. I offer you, now, all of the good that I shall do and I promise to accept, for love of you, all of the difficulty that I shall meet. Help me to conduct myself during this day in a manner pleasing to you. Amen.

We sanctify thy Name

George Wither

Our Father which in Heaven art,
We sanctify thy Name;
Thy Kingdom come, thy will be done,
In Heaven and Earth the same.
Give us this day, our daily bread,
And us forgive thou so,
As we on them that us offend,
Forgiveness do bestow.
Into temptation lead us not,
And us from evil free,
For thine the Kingdom, Power and Praise,
Is and shall ever be.

Children of quietness

Clement of Alexandria

O God, make us children of quietness and heirs of peace.

Deprive me not of your heavenly blessings

John Chrysostom, according to the hours of the day and night

1 O Lord, deprive me not of your heavenly blessings;

2 O Lord, deliver me from eternal torment;

3 O Lord, if I have sinned in my mind or thought, in word or deed, forgive me.

4 O Lord, deliver me from every ignorance and inattention, from a petty soul and a stony, hard heart;

5 O Lord, deliver me from every temptation;

6 O Lord, lighten my heart darkened by evil desires;

7 O Lord, I, being a human being, have sinned; you, being God, forgive me in your loving kindness, for you know the weakness of my soul.

8 O Lord, send down your grace to help me, that I may glorify your holy name;

9 O Lord Jesus Christ, write the name of your servant in the Book of Life, and grant me a blessed end;

10 O Lord my God, even if I have done nothing good in your sight, yet grant me your grace, that I may make a start doing good.

11 O Lord, sprinkle on my heart the dew of your grace;

12 O Lord of heaven and earth, remember me, your sinful servant, with my cold and impure heart, in your kingdom.

13 O Lord, receive me in repentance;

14 O Lord, do not leave me;

15 O Lord, save me from temptation;

16 O Lord, grant me pure thoughts;

17 O Lord, grant me tears of repentance, remembrance of death, and the sense of peace;

18 O Lord, make me remember to confess my sins;

19 O Lord, grant me humility, love, and obedience;

20 O Lord, grant me tolerance, magnanimity, and gentleness;

21 O Lord, implant in me the root of all blessings: the reverence of you in my heart;

22 O Lord, grant that I may love you with all my heart and soul, and that I may obey your will in all things;

23 O Lord, shield me from evil people, devils and passions;
24 O Lord, you know your creation and what you have planned
   for it; may your will also be fulfilled in me, a sinner, for you
   are blessed for evermore. Amen.

New every morning

John Keble

New every morning is the love
Our wakening and uprising prove;
Through sleep and darkness safely brought,
Restored to life, and power, and thought.

New mercies, each returning day,
Hover around us while we pray;
New perils past, new sins forgiven,
New thoughts of God, new hopes of heaven.

If on our daily course our mind
Be set to hallow all we find,
New treasures still, of countless price,
God will provide for sacrifice.

The trivial round, the common task,
Would furnish all we ought to ask,
Room to deny ourselves, a road
To bring us daily nearer God.

Only, O Lord, in thy dear love
Fit us for perfect rest above;
And help us this and every day
To live more nearly as we pray.

A morning hymn

Thomas Ken
Awake, my soul, and with the sun
Thy daily stage of duty run;
Shake off dull sloth, and early rise
To pay thy morning sacrifice.

Redeem thy misspent time that's past;
Live this day as if 'twere thy last;
T'improve thy talent take due care:
'Gainst the great day thyself prepare.

Let all thy converse be sincere,
Thy conscience as the noonday clear;
Think how all-seeing God thy ways
And all thy secret thoughts surveys.

Influenced by the light divine
Let thy own light in good works shine:
Reflect all heaven's propitious ways,
In ardent love and cheerful praise.

Wake, and lift up thyself, my heart,
And with the angels bear thy part,
Who all night long unwearied sing
Glory to the eternal king.

I wake, I wake, ye heavenly choir;
May your devotion me inspire,
That I like you my age may spend,
Like you may on my God attend.

May I like you in God delight,
Have all day long my God in sight,
Perform like you my Maker's will;
Oh may I never more do ill!

Had I your wings, to heaven I'd fly;
But God shall that defect supply,
And my soul, winged with warm desire,
Shall all day long to heaven aspire.

Glory to Thee who safe has kept,
And hath refreshed me whilst I slept.
Grant, Lord, when I from death shall wake,
I may of endless light partake.

I would not wake, nor rise again,
Even heaven itself I would disdain,
Wert not Thou there to be enjoyed,
And I in hymns to be employed.

Heaven is, dear Lord, where'er Thou art:
Oh never, then, from me depart;
For to my soul 'tis hell to be
But for one moment without Thee.

Lord, I my vows to Thee renew;
Disperse my sins as morning dew;
Guard my first springs of thought and will,
And with Thyself my spirit fill.

Direct, control, suggest, this day,
All I design, or do, or say,
That all my powers, with all their might,
In Thy sole glory may unite.

This night

The Treasury of Devotion

God the Father bless me;
Jesus Christ defend and keep me;
the power of the Holy Spirit enlighten me and sanctify me,
this night and for ever.

An evening prayer

Thomas Ken

Glory to thee, my God, this night
for all the blessings of the light;
keep me, O keep me, King of kings,
beneath thy own almighty wings.

Praise God, from whom all blessings flow,
praise him, all creatures here below,
praise him above, ye heavenly host,
praise Father, Son, and Holy Ghost.

Our sleeping bodies

R.L. Stevenson

We resign into your hands our sleeping bodies, our cold hearths and open doors. Give us to awaken with smiles, give us to labour smiling. As the sun returns in the east, so let our patience be renewed with dawn; as the sun lightens the world, so let our loving kindness make bright this house of our habitation.

Prayer of solace

Attributed to J.H. Newman
May Christ support us all the day long, till the shadows lengthen, and the evening comes, and the busy world is hushed, and the fever of life is over and our work is done. Then in his mercy may he give us a safe lodging, and holy rest and peace at the last. Amen.

I will lay down in peace

The Treasury of Devotion
Into your hands, O Lord, I commend my spirit, for you have redeemed me, O Lord, the God of truth. I will lay down in peace, and take my rest, for it is you, Lord, only who make me live in safety.

In the evening of life

Lutheran Manual of Prayer
Abide with us, O Lord, for it is toward evening and the day is far spent; abide with us, and with your whole church. Abide with us in the evening of the day, in the evening of life, in the evening of the world. Abide with us and with all your faithful ones, O Lord, in time and eternity.

Waking or sleeping

Traditional Irish
Be thou my vision, O Lord of my heart;
Naught be all else to me, save that thou art,
Thou my best thought, by day or by night,
Waking or sleeping, thy presence my light.

In your light we may see light

Lancelot Andrewes

Lord God, you have sent out your light, created the morning, and have made the sun to rise on the good and the evil; enlighten the blindness of our minds with the knowledge of the truth. Pour out the light of your countenance on us, that in your light we may see light, and, at the last, see the light of your grace and the light of your glory.

Make me, O my God

Thomas Aquinas

Make me, O my God,
humble without pretence,
cheerful without levity,
serious without dejection,
grave without moroseness,
active without frivolity,
truthful without duplicity,
fearful of thee without despair,
trustful of thee without presumption,
chaste without depravity,
able to correct my neighbour without angry feeling,
and by word and example to edify him without pride,
obedient without gainsaying,
patient without murmuring.

Preserve and keep us

Martin Luther, his morning prayer

We give thanks to you, heavenly Father, through Jesus Christ your dear Son, that you have protected us through the night from all danger and harm; and we beseech you to preserve and keep us, this day also, from all sin and evil; that in all our thoughts, words

and deeds, we may serve and please you. In your hands we commend our bodies and souls, and all that is ours. Let your holy
angel guard us, that the wicked one may have no power over us.

All those that love me

From an old New England sampler
God bless all those that I love;
God bless all those that love me.
God bless all those that love those that I love
And all those that love those that love me.

Guide and sanctify us

Philipp Melanchthon, his morning prayer
Almighty, eternal God, Father of our Lord Jesus Christ, creator of
heaven and earth and mankind, together with your Son, our Lord
Jesus Christ, your Word and Image, and with your Holy Spirit:
Have mercy on us, and forgive us all our sins for your Son's sake,
whom you have made our Mediator. Guide and sanctify us by
your Holy Spirit, who was poured out on the apostles. Grant that
we may truly know and praise you throughout eternity.

As pants the hart for cooling streams

Nahum Tate and Nicholas Brady, based on Psalm 42
As pants the hart for cooling streams,
When heated in the chase,
So longs my soul, O God, for Thee
And Thy refreshing grace.

For Thee, my God, the living God,
My thirsty soul doth pine;
O, when shall I behold Thy face,
Thou majesty divine?

Why restless, why cast down, my soul?
Hope still; and thou shalt sing
The praise of Him Who is thy God,
Thy health's eternal spring.

To Father, Son, and Holy Ghost,
The God Whom we adore,
Be glory as it was, is now,
And shall be evermore.

Make this day peaceful

Traditional Gaelic prayer
Lord, you commanded peace:
you gave peace.
You bequeathed peace;
give us your peace from heaven.
Make this day peaceful,
and the remaining days of our life.

That I may rest in you

E.B. Pusey
Good Jesus, strength of the weary, rest of the restless, by the
weariness and unrest of your sacred cross, come to me who am
weary that I may rest in you.

Teach me the art of patience while I am well

Thomas Fuller

Lord, teach me the art of patience while I am well, and enable me to use of it when I am sick. In that day either lighten my burden or strengthen my back. Make me, who so often in my health have discovered my weakness in presuming on my own strength, to be strong in my sickness when I solely rely on your assistance.

The same kindness toward me this day

Thomas Becon

Heavenly Father, I most heartily thank thee, that it has pleased thy fatherly goodness to take care of me this night past. I most entirely beseech thee, most merciful Father, to show the same kindness toward me this day, in preserving my body and soul; that I may neither think, breathe, speak, nor do anything that may be displeasing to thy fatherly goodness, dangerous to myself, or hurtful to my neighbour; but that all my doings may be agreeable to your most blessed will, which is always good; that they may advance thy glory, answer to my vocation, and profit my neighbour, whom I ought to love as myself; that, whenever thou callest me hence, I may be found the child not of darkness but of light; through Jesus Christ our Lord.

The light of the morning

Book of Hours, 1864

O Lord, who has brought us through the darkness of night to the light of the morning, and who by your Holy Spirit illumines the darkness of ignorance and sin: We beseech you, from your loving kindness, pour your holy light into our souls; that we may always be devoted to you, by whose wisdom we were created, by whose mercy we were redeemed, and by whose providence we are governed; to the honour and glory of your great name.

Guard us in our going out and coming in

Author unknown

God Almighty bless us with his Holy Spirit this day;
guard us in our going out and coming in;
keep us always steadfast in his faith,
free from sin and safe from danger;
through Jesus Christ our Lord.

We your unworthy children on earth pray

Miles Coverdale

O Lord God, *our Father in heaven,* we your unworthy children on earth pray that you will look on us in your mercy, and give us your grace; that *your holy name* may be sanctified among us and in all the world, through the pure and sincere teaching of the Word, and through earnest charity in our daily living and our conversation. Root out from us all false teaching and evil living, so that your name is not slandered.

Let *your kingdom come,* and be great. May all sinful, blind people who are in the devil's grip be brought to the knowledge of the true faith in Jesus Christ your Son.

Strengthen us, Lord, with your Spirit, to do and to suffer *your will* both in life and death, so that our will may always be broken, offered and put to death.

And *give us our daily bread.* Preserve us from covetous desire so that we may be assured of having the abundance of all good things.

Forgive us our trespasses, as we forgive those who offend us, that our heart may have a sure and glad conscience, and that we may never fear, or be afraid of any sin.

Lead us not into temptation, but help us through your Spirit to subdue the flesh, to despise the world with its vanities, and to overcome the devil with all his cunning attacks.

And finally, *deliver us from all evil,* physical and spiritual, temporal and eternal.

Teach us

Desiderius Erasmus
Almighty God, teach us by your holy Spirit, what to believe, what to do, and where to take our rest.

Awake in the duties of our callings

John Donne
Keep us, Lord, so awake in the duties of our callings that we may sleep in your peace and wake in your glory.

Enlighten my heart

John Chrysostom
O Lord, enlighten my heart, which evil desire has darkened. O Lord, help me to think about what is good.

And in thy presence rest

Bernard of Clairvaux, translated by Edward Caswell
Jesus, the very thought of thee
With sweetness fills the breast;
But sweeter far thy face to see,
And in thy presence rest.

Every day is Thy gift

Dr Johnson
Make me remember, O God, that every day is Thy gift and ought to be used according to Thy command, through Jesus Christ our Lord.

You have today, and every day of your life

Christopher Smart

Remember, Christian soul,
that you have today,
and every day of your life:
God to glorify,
Jesus to imitate,
a soul to save,
a body to mortify,
sins to repent of,
virtues to acquire,
hell to avoid,
heaven to gain,
eternity to prepare for,
time to profit by,
neighbours to edify,
the world to despise,
devils to combat,
passions to subdue,
death, perhaps, to suffer,
judgement to undergo.

Altogether absorbed in the abyss of your love

Anselm

O my Saviour, and my God, let it come. May the hour come when my eyes are given the vision of what I already believe, and grasp what I now hope for and greet from a distance. May my spirit embrace and kiss what now with my whole might I yearn for, and be altogether absorbed in the abyss of your love. But meanwhile bless, my soul, my Saviour, and praise his name, which is holy and full of the holiest delights.

Keep our going out and our coming in

After Psalm 121:8 NRSV

May the Lord keep our going out and our coming in from this time on and for evermore.

Love, power, joy

William Temple

May the love of the Lord Jesus draw us to Himself;
may the power of the Lord Jesus strengthen us in His service;
may the joy of the Lord Jesus fill our souls.
May the blessing of God almighty, the Father, the Son and the Holy
*   Ghost,*
be amongst us and remain with us always.

Teach us to number our days

Thomas Chalmers

Lord, teach us to number our days, that we may apply our hearts to wisdom.

Lighten, if it is your will, the pressures of this world's cares.

Above all, reconcile us to your will, and give us a peace which the world cannot take away; through our Saviour Jesus Christ.

Wisdom

Attributed to Reinhold Niebuhr; also known as 'The Serenity Prayer'
God, give us the serenity to accept what cannot be changed;
give us the courage to change what should be changed;
give us the wisdom to distinguish one from the other.

God be in my head

From a Book of Hours, *a 1514 service book used in Clare*
College, Cambridge
God be in my head
and in my understanding;
God be in my eyes
and in my looking;
God be in my mouth
and in my speaking;
God be in my heart
and in my thinking;
God be at my end
and at my departing.

Pure, gentle, truthful

Charles Kingsley
Guide us, teach us, and strengthen us, O Lord, we beseech thee,
until we become such as thou wouldest have us be: pure, gentle,
truthful, high-minded, courteous, generous, able, dutiful and useful; for thy honour and glory.

Grace, love, favour

John Newton
May the grace of Christ our Saviour,
And the Father's boundless love,
With the Holy Spirit's favour,
Rest upon us from above.

To live more nearly as we pray

John Keble
And help us, this day and every day,
To live more nearly as we pray.

A contrite and humbled heart

Gallican Sacramentary
Give us, O Lord, purity of lips, clean and innocent hearts, and rectitude of action; give us humility, patience, self-wisdom and understanding, the spirit of counsel and strength, the spirit of knowledge and godliness, and of thy fear; make us ever to seek thy face with all our heart, all our soul, all our mind; grant us to have a contrite and humbled heart in thy presence, to prefer nothing to thy love. Have mercy upon us, we humbly beseech thee; through Jesus Christ our Lord.

In little daily duties

Christina Rossetti
Grant us, we beseech thee, O Lord, grace to follow thee whithersoever thou goest.

In little daily duties to which thou callest us, bow down our wills to simple obedience, patience under pain or provocation, strict truthfulness of word or manner, humility and kindness.

In great acts of duty or perfection, if thou shouldst call us to them, uplift us to sacrifice and heroic courage, that in all things, both small and great, we may be imitators of thy dear Son, even Jesus Christ our Lord.

That my joy may be full

Anselm
My God,
I pray that I may so know you and love you
that I may rejoice in you.
And if I may not do so fully in this life
let me go steadily on
to the day when I come to that fullness ...
Let me receive
That which you promised through your truth,
that my joy may be full.

PART THREE

EVERYDAY LIFE

Nature
Glory be to God for dappled things

Gerard Manley Hopkins, 'Pied Beauty'
Glory be to God for dappled things —
For skies of couple-colour as a brinded cow;
For rose-moles all in stipple upon trout that swim;
Fresh-firecoal chestnut-falls; finches' wings;
Landscape plotted and pieced — fold, fallow and plough;
And áll trádes, their gear and tackle and trim.
All things counter, original, spare, strange;
Whatever is fickle, freckled (who knows how?)
With swift, slow; sweet, sour; adazzle, dim;
He fathers-forth whose beauty is past change:
Praise him.

Simple beauty

Robert Browning
If you get simple beauty and naught else, you get about the best thing God invents.

Apprehensions of the world

Thomas Traherne, Centuries of Meditations

Will you see the infancy of this sublime and celestial greatness? Those pure and virgin apprehensions I had from the womb, and that divine light wherewith I was born, are the best unto this day wherein I can see the universe. By the gift of God they attended me into the world, and by His special favour I remember them till now. Verily they seem the greatest gifts His wisdom could bestow, for without them all other gifts had been dead and vain. They are unattainable by book, and therefore I will teach them by experience. Pray for them earnestly: for they will make you angelical, and wholly celestial. Certainly Adam in Paradise had not more sweet and curious apprehensions of the world, than I when I was a child ...

The corn was orient and immortal wheat, which never should be reaped, nor was ever sown. I thought it had stood from ever-lasting to everlasting. The dust and stones of the street were as precious as gold. The gates were at first the end of the world. The green trees when I saw them first through one of the gates trans-ported and ravished me; their sweetness and unusual beauty made my heart to leap, and almost mad with ecstasy, they were such strange and wonderful things. The men! O what venerable and reverend creatures did the aged seem! Immortal cherubim! And young men glittering and sparkling angels, and maids strange seraphic pieces of life and beauty! Boys and girls tumbling in the street, and playing, were moving jewels. I knew not that they were born and should die. But all things abided eternally, as they were in their proper places. Eternity was manifest in the light of the day, and something infinite behind everything appeared, which talked with my expectation and moved my desire. The city seemed to stand in Eden, or to be built in Heaven. The streets were mine, the temple was mine, the people were mine, their clothes and gold and silver were mine, as much as their sparkling eyes, fair skins, and ruddy faces. The skies were mine, and so were the sun and moon and stars, and all the world was mine, and I the only spectator and enjoyer of it. I knew no churlish proprieties, nor bounds, nor divisions; but all proprieties and divisions were mine: all treasures and the possessors of them. So that with much ado I was corrupted; and made to learn the dirty devices of this world. Which now I unlearn, and become as it were a little child again, that I may enter into the Kingdom of God.

The operation of God

William Temple
Jesus taught men to see the operation of God in the regular and the normal – in the rising of the sun and the falling of the rain and the growth of the plant.

God's handwriting

Charles Kingsley
Beauty is God's handwriting. Welcome it in every fair face, every fair day, every fair flower.

Beyond all creatures

Christina Rossetti
Lord, purge our eyes to see
Within the seed a tree,
Within the glowing egg a bird,
Within the shroud a butterfly.
Till, taught by such we see
Beyond all creatures, Thee.

For the beauty of the earth

F.S. Pierpoint
For the beauty of the earth,
For the beauty of the skies,
For the love which from our birth
Over and around us lies:
Christ, our God, to thee we raise
This our sacrifice of praise.

For the beauty of each hour
Of the day and of the night,
Hill and vale and tree and flower,
Sun and moon and stars of light:
Christ, our God, to thee we raise
This our sacrifice of praise.

For our mother the earth

Francis of Assisi, 'Canticle of the Sun'
Most high, most great and good Lord, to you belong praises, glory and every blessing; to you alone do they belong, most high God.

May you be blessed, my Lord, for the gift of all your creatures and especially for our brother sun, by whom the day is enlightened. He is radiant and bright, of great splendour, bearing witness to you, O my God.

May you be blessed, my Lord, for our sister the moon and the stars; you have created them in the heavens, fair and clear.

May you be blessed, my Lord, for my brother the wind, for the air, for cloud and calm, for every kind of weather, for through them you sustain all creatures.

May you be blessed, my Lord, for our sister water, which is very useful, humble, pure and precious.

May you be blessed, my Lord, for our brother fire, bright, noble and beautiful, untamable and strong, by whom you illumine the night.

May you be blessed, my Lord, for our mother the earth, who sustains and nourishes us, who brings forth all kinds of fruit, herbs and brightly coloured flowers.

May you be blessed, my Lord, for those who pardon out of love for you, and who patiently bear illness and tribulation.

Happy are those who abide in peace, for through you, most high God, they will be crowned.

May you be blessed, my Lord, for our sister death of body, from whom no living person can escape. Woe to him who dies in a state of mortal sin. Happy are those who at the hour of death are found in obedience to your holy will, for the second death cannot hurt them.

Praise and bless, my Lord; give him thanks and serve him with great humility.

Ambition and Guidance
A guiding star

St Columba
My dearest Lord,
be Thou a bright flame before me,
be Thou a guiding star above me,
be Thou a smooth path beneath me,
be Thou a kindly shepherd behind me,
today and evermore.

We'll trust him for all that's to come

Joseph Hart
How good is the God we adore,
Our faithful, unchangeable Friend!
His love is as great as his power,
And knows neither measure nor end!
'Tis Jesus, the First and the Last,
Whose Spirit shall guide us safe home:

We'll praise him for all that is past,
We'll trust him for all that's to come.

God guide me

Traditional Gaelic prayer
God guide me with your wisdom,
God help me with your mercy,
God protect me with your strength,
God fill me with your grace,
for the sake of your anointed Son.

Be thou my guide

Horatius Bonar
Thy way, not mine, O Lord,
However dark it be:
Lead me by thine own hand,
Choose out the path for me.

The kingdom that I seek
Is thine: so let the way
That leads to it be thine,
Else I must surely stray.

Take thou my cup, and it
With joy or sorrow fill,
As best to thee may seem;
Choose thou my good and ill.

Not mine, not mine the choice
In things or great or small;
Be thou my guide, my strength,
My wisdom and my all.

Cause me to know

Henry Martyn

Lord, I am blind and helpless, stupid and ignorant: cause me to hear; cause me to know; teach me to do; lead me.

Eyes for all your truth

Søren Kierkegaard

Lord, give us weak eyes for things which are of no account and clear eyes for all your truth.

The guidance of your wisdom

Author unknown

Grant us, Lord, to know in weakness the strength of your incarnation:
> in pain the triumph of your passion:
> in poverty the riches of your Godhead:
> in reproach the satisfaction of your sympathy:
> in loneliness the comfort of your continual presence:
> in difficulty the efficacy of your intercession:
> in perplexity the guidance of your wisdom;
> and by your glorious death and resurrection bring us at last to the joy of seeing you face to face.

Birthdays, New Year and Times of Life
My Baptismal Birthday

Samuel Taylor Coleridge

Coleridge wrote that this poem was 'composed on a sick-bed, under severe bodily suffering, on my spiritual birthday, 28 October'.

God's child in Christ adopted, – Christ my all, –
What that earth boasts were not lost cheaply, rather
Than forfeit that blest name, by which I call
The Holy One, the Almighty God, my Father? –
Father! in Christ we live, and Christ in Thee –
Eternal Thou, and everlasting we.
The heir of heaven, henceforth I fear not death:
In Christ I live! in Christ I draw the breath
Of the true life! – Let then earth, sea, and sky
Make war against me! On my heart I show
Their mighty master's seal. In vain they try
To end my life, that can but end its woe. –
Is that a death-bed where a Christian lies? –
Yes! but not his – 'tis Death itself there dies.

New Year

Thomas Tusser

Give us the will, O God,
to pray to thee continually,
to learn to know thee rightfully,
to serve thee always holily,
to ask thee all things needfully,
to praise thee always worthily,
to love thee always steadfastly,
to ask thy mercy heartily,
to trust thee always faithfully,
to obey him always willingly,
to abide him always patiently,
to use thy neighbour honestly,
to live here always virtuously,
to help the poor in misery,
to thank thee ever gratefully,
to hope for heaven's felicity,
to have faith, hope and charity.

Wisdom to redeem the time

Christina Rossetti

O Lord God of time and eternity, who makes us creatures of
time, that when time is over, we may attain your blessed eternity:
With time, your gift, give us also wisdom to redeem the time, so
our day of grace is not lost; for our Lord Jesus' sake.

I again dedicate my whole self to Thee

David Livingstone, Last Journal, 19 March 1872, his birthday

My Jesus, my King, my Life, my All; I again dedicate my whole
self to Thee. Accept me, and grant, O gracious Father, that ere this
year is gone I may finish my task. In Jesus' name I ask it. Amen,
so let it be.

Student days: faith and fruitful study

King's College, Cambridge

Almighty Father, grant that our universities and colleges may be
houses of faith and fruitful study; and that their students may so
learn truth as to bear its light along all their ways, and so learn
Christ as to be found in him; who liveth and reigneth with thee
and the Holy Spirit, one God, world without end.

To all students

Thomas à Kempis

Grant, O Lord, to all students, to know what is worth knowing,
to love what is worth loving, to praise what delights you most, to
value what is precious in your sight and to reject what is evil in
your eyes. Grant them true discernment to distinguish between
different things. Above all, may they search out and do what is
most pleasing to you; through Jesus Christ our Lord.

Student days: fill me with the spirit of intelligence and wisdom

Alcuin

Give me grace, Lord, to be strong, prudent, just and wise in all things. Give me an exact faith, generous love and unshakeable trust in you. Fill me with the spirit of intelligence and wisdom. Let me always be considerate about other people. O perfect and eternal Light, enlighten me.

Student days: Streams of knowledge

Alcuin

Good Lord, you have refreshed our souls with the streams of knowledge; lead us at last to yourself, the source and spring of knowledge.

Marriage and Home Life
Unless the Lord builds

Psalm 127:1 NRSV
Unless the LORD builds the house,
  those who build it labour in vain.

Live together in holy love

John Knox
The Lord make you holy and bless you, the Lord pour the riches of his grace on you, that you may please him, and live together in holy love to your lives' end.

My hearth, my home

Traditional Hebridean chant
The Sacred Three
My fortress be
Encircling me
Come and be round
My hearth, my home.

May you be rich in blessings

Author unknown, old wedding blessing
May God be with you and bless you.
May you see your children's children.
May you be poor in misfortune, rich in blessings.
May you know nothing but happiness
From this day forward.

Sickness
Restore me to my health

Thomas Ken
Lord, bless all means that are used for my recovery, and restore me to my health in your good time; but if you have appointed that it should be otherwise, your blessed will be done. Draw me away from an affection for things below, and fill me with an ardent desire for heaven. Lord, fit me for yourself, and then call me to those joys unspeakable and full of glory, when it pleases you, and that for the sake of your only Son, Jesus, my Saviour.

On his Blindness

John Milton

When I consider how my light is spent
  Ere half my days, in this dark world and wide,
  And that one talent which is death to hide
  Lodged with me useless, though my soul more bent
To serve therewith my Maker, and present
  My true account, lest he returning chide:
  'Doth God exact day-labour, light denied?'
  I fondly ask. But patience, to prevent
That murmur, soon replies: 'God doth not need
  Either man's work or his own gifts, who best
  Bear his mild yoke, they serve him best, his State
Is Kingly. Thousands at his bidding speed
  And post o'er land and ocean without rest;
  They also serve, who only stand and wait.'

Healing power

Mozarabic Liturgy
O Lord God of our salvation, to whom no sickness is incurable, we pray that in your compassion you will drive away from your servants, who look for your heavenly medicine, all illness; show forth in them the might of your healing power, and make them whole both in body and soul; through Jesus Christ our Lord.

Mental illness

William Cowper, from The Task
Cowper suffered from severe depression and contemplated suicide on a number of occasions.

I was a stricken deer, that left the herd
Long since; with many an arrow deep infixt

My panting side was charg'd, when I withdrew
To seek a tranquil death in distant shades.
There was I found by One who had Himself
Been hurt by th'archers. In His side He bore,
And in His hands and feet, the cruel scars.
With gentle force soliciting the darts,
He drew them forth, and heal'd, and bade me live.
Since then, with few associates, in remote
And silent woods, I wander, far from those
My former partners of the peopled scene;
With few associates, and not wishing more.

Stress
Hope in God

Psalm 42:11 NRSV
Why are you cast down, O my soul,
   and why are you disquieted within me?
Hope in God; for I shall again praise him,
   my help and my God.

In times of stress

After Margery Kempe
Blessed Jesus, you are always near in times of stress.
Although we cannot feel your presence you are close.
You are always there to help and watch over us.
Nothing in heaven or on earth can separate you from us.

Calm the waves of this heart

Søren Kierkegaard
O Lord, calm the waves of this heart, calm its tempest!
   Calm yourself, O my soul, so that the divine can act in you!

Calm yourself, O my soul, so that God is able to repose in you, so that his peace may cover you!

Yes, Father in heaven, often have we found that the world cannot give us peace, but make us feel that you are able to give us peace; let us know the truth of your promise: that the whole world may not be able to take away your peace.

The breastplate

St Patrick

I bind unto myself today
The power of God to hold and lead,
His eye to watch, his might to stay,
His ear to hearken to my need.
The wisdom of my God to teach,
His hand to guide, his shield to ward;
The word of God to give me speech,
His heavenly host to be my guard.

Christ be with me, Christ within me,
Christ behind me, Christ before me,
Christ beside me, Christ to win me,
Christ to comfort and restore me,
Christ beneath me, Christ above me,
Christ in quiet, Christ in danger,
Christ in mouth of friend and stranger.

I bind unto myself the name,
The strong name of the Trinity;
By invocation of the same,
The Three in One, the One in Three,
Of whom all nature hath creation;
Eternal Father, Spirit, Word,
Praise to the Lord of my salvation,
Salvation is of Christ the Lord.

Omnipotent and omniscient Love

William Law, A Serious Call to a Devout and Holy Life
To know that Love alone was the beginning of nature and creature, that nothing but Love encompasses the whole universe of things, that the governing hand that overrules all, the watchful Eye that sees through all, is nothing but omnipotent and omniscient Love, using an infinity of wisdom, to save every misguided creature from the miserable works of his own hands, and make happiness and glory the perpetual inheritance of all the creation, is a reflection that must be quite ravishing to every intelligent creature that is sensible of it.

Fear and Times of Change
My boat is small

Breton fisherman's prayer
Protect me, dear Lord;
My boat is so small,
And your sea is so big.

Whom shall I fear?

Psalm 27:1, 13–14 NRSV
The LORD is my light and my salvation;
whom shall I fear?
The LORD is the stronghold of my life;
of whom shall I be afraid?...

I believe that I shall see the goodness of the LORD
in the land of the living.
Wait for the LORD;
be strong, and let your heart take courage;
wait for the LORD!

O God, our Help in ages past

Isaac Watts

O God, our Help in ages past,
Our Hope for years to come,
Our Shelter from the stormy blast,
And our eternal Home!

Beneath the shadow of Thy throne
Thy saints have dwelt secure;
Sufficient is Thine arm alone,
And our defence is sure.

Before the hills in order stood,
Or Earth received her frame,
From everlasting Thou art God,
To endless years the same.

Thy Word commands our flesh to dust:
'Return, ye sons of men!'
All nations rose from earth at first
And turn to earth again.

A thousand ages in Thy sight
Are like an evening gone;
Short as the watch that ends the night
Before the rising sun.

The busy tribes of flesh and blood,
With all their cares and fears,
Are carried downward by the flood,
And lost in following years.

Time, like an ever rolling stream,
Bears all its sons away;
They fly forgotten as a dream
Dies at the opening day.

Like flowery fields the nations stand,
Pleased with the morning light;
The flowers beneath the mower's hand
Lie withering ere 'tis night.

O God our help in ages past,
Our hope for years to come,
Be Thou our guard while life shall last,
And our eternal Home.

Which casts out all fear

E.B. Pusey
Most loving Lord, give me a childlike love of thee, which casts
out all fear.

Psalm 23

George Herbert, The Temple
The God of love my shepherd is,
  And he that doth me feed:
While he is mine, and I am His,
  What can I want or need?

He leads me to the tender grass,
  Where I both feed and rest;
Then to the streams that gently pass:
  In both I have the best.

Or if I stray, he doth convert,
  And bring my mind in frame:
And all this not for my desert,
  But for his holy name.

Yea, in death's shady, black abode
  Well may I walk, not fear:
For thou art with me, and thy rod
  To guide, thy staff to bear.

Nay, thou dost make me sit and dine,
  Even in my enemies' sight;
My head with oil, my cup with wine
  Runs over day and night.

Surely thy sweet and wondrous love
  Shall measure all my days;
And as it never shall remove,
  So neither shall my praise.

The changing scenes of life

Nahum Tate and Nicholas Brady
Through all the changing scenes of life,
In trouble and in joy,
The praises of my God shall still
My heart and tongue employ.

Drives away his fear

John Newton
How sweet the name of Jesus sounds
  In a believer's ear!
It soothes his sorrows, heals his wounds,
  And drives away his fear.

It makes the wounded spirit whole,
  And calms the troubled breast;
'Tis manna to the hungry soul,
  And to the weary rest.

Through all our life be near us

Martin Rinkart, translated by Catherine Winkworth
Now thank we all our God,
With heart and hand and voices,
Who wondrous things has done,
In whom his world rejoices;
Who from our mother's arms
Has blessed us on our way
With countless gifts of love
And still is ours today.

O may this bounteous God
Through all our life be near us,
With ever joyful hearts
And blessed peace to cheer us;
And keep us in his grace,
And guide us when perplexed,
And free us from all ills
In this world and the next.

Each fear, each fret, each care

Horatius Bonar
Fill Thou my life, O Lord my God,
In every part with praise,
That my whole being may proclaim
Thy being and Thy ways.
Not for the lip of praise alone,
Nor e'en the praising heart
I ask, but for a life made up
Of praise in every part!

Fill every part of me with praise;
Let all my being speak
Of Thee and of Thy love, O Lord,

Poor though I be, and weak.
So shalt Thou, Lord, from me, e'en me,
Receive the glory due;
And so shall I begin on earth
The song forever new.

So shall each fear, each fret, each care
Be turned into a song,
And every winding of the way
The echo shall prolong;
So shall no part of day or night
From sacredness be free;
But all my life, in every step
Be fellowship with Thee.

Worry and Difficulties
My stronghold

David, 2 Samuel 22:1 NRSV
The LORD is my rock, my fortress, and my deliverer,
    my God, my rock, in whom I take refuge,
my shield and the horn of my salvation,
    my stronghold and my refuge,
    my saviour; you save me from violence.

Put away from my heart all useless anxiety

Thomas à Kempis
Strengthen me, O God, by the grace of your Holy Spirit; grant
me to be strengthened with the might of the inner man, and to
put away from my heart all useless anxiety and distress, and let me
never be distracted by various longings, whether they are worthless or precious; but may I view all things as passing away, and
myself as passing away with them.

Grant me prudently to avoid the one who flatters me, and patiently to bear with the one who contradicts me; for it is a mark of great wisdom not to be moved by every wind of words or to be influenced by wicked flattery; for thus we will go on securely in the course we have begun.

Keep us in all perplexity

Francis Paget

Set free, O Lord, the souls of your servants from all restlessness and anxiety. Give us that peace and power which flow from you. Keep us in all perplexity and distress, that upheld by your strength and stayed on the rock of your faithfulness we may abide in you now and evermore.

Teresa's Bookmark

Teresa of Avila *1515-82 Spanish Carmelite Mystic*

*Let nothing disturb you
nothing frighten you,
all things are passing;
patient endurance
attains all things.
One whom God possesses
lacks nothing,
for God alone suffices.*

Anxious about nothing

B.F. Westcott

O Lord God, in whom we live and move and have our being, open our eyes that we may behold your fatherly presence always with us. Draw our hearts to you with the power of your love. Teach us to be anxious about nothing, and when we have done what you have given us to do, help us, O God our Saviour, to leave the issue to your wisdom. Take from us all doubt and mistrust. Lift our hearts up to you in heaven, and make us to know that all things are possible for us through your Son our Redeemer.

The anxious cravings of my heart

Søren Kierkegaard
To thee, O God, we turn for peace. Grant us the blessed assurance that nothing shall deprive us of that peace, neither ourselves, nor our foolish earthly desires, nor my wild longings, nor the anxious cravings of my heart.

All storm-tossed souls

Basil the Great
O Lord our God, teach us to ask aright for the right blessings. Guide the vessel of our life towards yourself, the tranquil haven of all storm-tossed souls. Show us the course we should take. Renew a willing spirit within us. Let your Spirit curb our wayward senses and guide and enable us to what is our true good, to keep your laws and in all our deeds always to rejoice in your glorious and gladdening presence. For yours is the glory and praise of all your saints for ever and ever.

Free from all anxious thoughts

Augustine
Almighty God, who knows our necessities before we ask, and our ignorance in asking: Set free your servants from all anxious thoughts about tomorrow; make us content with your good gifts; and confirm our faith that as we seek your kingdom, you will not allow us to lack any good thing; through Jesus Christ our Lord.

Dangers and deliverance

Leonine Sacramentary

Grant, we pray, Lord our God, that in whatever dangers we are placed we may call on your name, and that when deliverance comes from on high we may never cease from praising you; through Jesus Christ our Lord.

Persecution and Opposition
A very present help in trouble

Thomas à Kempis

Write your blessed name, O Lord, upon my heart, there to remain so indelibly engraved, that no prosperity, no adversity shall ever move me from your love. Be to me a strong tower of defence, a comforter in tribulation, a deliverer in distress, a very present help in trouble and a guide to heaven through the many temptations and dangers of this life.

Those who suffer for the testimony of the truth

John Knox

O God of all power, you called from death the great pastor of the sheep, our Lord Jesus: comfort and defend the flock which he has redeemed through the blood of the everlasting covenant. Increase the number of true preachers; enlighten the hearts of the ignorant; relieve the pain of the afflicted, especially of those who suffer for the testimony of the truth; by the power of our Lord Jesus Christ.

Work

My daily labour to pursue

Charles Wesley

Forth in your name, O Lord I go,
My daily labour to pursue,
You, only you, resolved to know
In all I think, or speak or do.

The task your wisdom has assigned
O let me cheerfully fulfil,
In all my works your presence find,
And prove your good and perfect will.

Thou knowest how busy I must be this day

General Lord Astley, before the battle of Edgehill

O Lord, thou knowest how busy I must be this day. If I forget thee, do not thou forget me.

I ask for strength equal to my tasks

Phillips Brooks

O Lord, I do not pray for tasks equal to my strength: I ask for strength equal to my tasks.

To do it as for thee

George Herbert

Teach me, my God and King,
in all things thee to see,
and what I do in anything
to do it as for thee.

A man that looks on glass
on it may stay his eye;
or if he pleaseth, through it pass,
and then the heaven espy.

All may of thee partake;
nothing can be so mean
which, with this tincture, 'For thy sake',
will not grow bright and clean.

A servant with this clause
makes drudgery divine:
who sweeps a room, as for thy laws,
makes that and the action fine.

This is the famous stone
that turneth all to gold:
for that which God doth touch and own
cannot for less be told.

Give us work

Traditional
O God, give us work
till our life shall end,
and give us life
till our work is done.

Our daily work

Thomas Arnold
O Lord, give our blessing, we pray, to our daily work, that we may do it in faith and heartily, as to the Lord and not to men.

All our powers of body and mind are yours, and we devote them to your service. Sanctify them, and the work in which we are engaged; and, Lord, so bless our efforts that they may bring forth in us the fruits of true wisdom.

Teach us to seek after truth and enable us to gain it; and grant that while we know earthly things, we may know you, and be known by you, through and in your Son Jesus Christ.

Serving God
The multitudes of the heathen

Francis Xavier
O God of all the nations of the earth, remember the multitudes of the heathen, who, though created in thine image, have not known thee, nor the dying of thy Son their Saviour Jesus Christ; and grant that by the prayers and labours of thy holy church they may be delivered from all superstition and unbelief and brought to worship thee; through him whom thou hast sent to be the resurrection and the life to all men, the same thy Son Jesus Christ our Lord.

He giveth power to the faint

Isaiah 40:1–2, 25–31 AV
Comfort ye, comfort ye my people, saith your God.

Speak ye comfortably to Jerusalem, and cry unto her, that her warfare is accomplished, that her iniquity is pardoned: for she hath received of the Lord's hand double for all her sins.

To whom then will ye liken me, or shall I be equal? saith the Holy One.

Lift up your eyes on high, and behold who hath created these things, that bringeth out their host by number: he calleth them all by names by the greatness of his might, for that he is strong in power; not one faileth.

Why sayest thou, O Jacob, and speakest, O Israel, My way is hid from the Lord, and my judgement is passed over from my God?

Hast thou not known? hast thou not heard, that the everlasting God, the Lord, the Creator of the ends of the earth, fainteth not, neither is weary? there is no searching of his understanding.

He giveth power to the faint; and to them that have no might he increaseth strength.

Even the youths shall faint and be weary, and the young men shall utterly fall:

But they that wait upon the Lord shall renew their strength; they shall mount up with wings as eagles; they shall run, and not be weary; and they shall walk, and not faint.

Serve Thee without failing

Anselm
Grant, Lord God, that we may cleave to Thee without parting,
worship Thee without wearying,
serve Thee without failing,
faithfully find Thee,
forever possess Thee,
the one only God, blessed for all eternity.

That we may fully serve Thee

From the Gelasian Sacramentary (based on a prayer by Augustine)
Eternal God,
the light of the minds that know Thee,
the life of the souls that love Thee,
the strength of the wills that serve Thee;
help us so to know Thee that we may truly love Thee,
so to love Thee that we may fully serve Thee,
whom to serve is perfect freedom.

I have nothing to do but to serve you

Richard Baxter

My Lord, I have nothing to do in this world but to seek and serve you.

I have nothing to do with my heart and its affections but to breathe after you.

I have nothing to do with my tongue and pen but to speak to you and for you, and to make known your glory and your will.

Know, love, follow

Richard of Chichester
Thanks be to Thee, Lord Jesus Christ,
for all the benefits which Thou hast won for us,
for all the pains and insults which Thou hast borne for us.
O most merciful Redeemer, Friend and Brother,
may we know Thee more clearly,
love Thee more dearly,
and follow Thee more nearly,
day by day.

Accept me and my service

David Livingstone

O Jesus, fill me with your love now, and I pray, accept me, and use me a little for your glory. O do, do, I pray, accept me and my service, and take all the glory.

No God but thee defend us

Martin Luther
In these our days so perilous,
Lord, peace in mercy send us;

No God but thee can fight for us,
No God but thee defend us;
Thou our only God and Saviour.

May we serve you in our daily lives

Boniface

Eternal God, the refuge of all your children,
in our weakness you are our strength,
in our darkness our light,
in our sorrow our comfort and peace.
May we always live in your presence,
and serve you in our daily lives;
through Jesus Christ our Lord.

Serving Others
Make me an instrument of your peace

Attributed to Francis of Assisi

Lord, make me an instrument of your peace.
Where there is hatred, let me sow love,
where there is injury, pardon,
where there is doubt, faith,
where there is despair, hope,
where there is darkness, light,
where there is sadness, joy.

O Divine Master, grant that we may not so much seek
to be consoled as to console,
not so much to be understood as to understand,
not so much to be loved as to love.
For it is in giving that we receive,
it is in pardoning that we are pardoned,
it is in dying that we are born to eternal life.

The needs and conditions of all

George Fox

O Lord, baptize our hearts into a sense of the needs and conditions of all.

Masters of ourselves

Alexander Paterson

Lord, help us to be masters of ourselves, that we may be servants of others.

Make us worthy, Lord, to serve our fellow-men

Mother Teresa

Make us worthy, Lord,
To serve our fellow-men
Throughout the world
Who live and die in poverty and hunger.
Give them, through our hands,
This day their daily bread;
And by our understanding love,
Give peace and joy.

You will require much from those to whom much is given

Augustine's Manual

O God, who has warned us that you will require much from those to whom much is given; grant that we, whose lot is cast in so goodly a heritage, may strive together the more abundantly, by prayer, by almsgiving, by fasting, and by all appointed means, to extend to those who do not know you what we so richly enjoy; and as we have entered into the labours of others so to labour that others may enter into ours, to the fulfilment of your holy will and the salvation of all mankind; through Jesus Christ our Lord.

Take my mouth to spread abroad the glory of your name

D.L. Moody

Use me, my Saviour, for whatever purpose and in what way you require. Here is my poor heart, an empty vessel: fill it with your grace. Here is my sinful and troubled soul: bring it to life and refresh it with your love. Take my heart for you to live in; my mouth to spread abroad the glory of your name; my love and all my powers for the advancement of your believing people; and never allow the steadfastness and confidence of my faith to abate.

Forgiving others

Prayer found near the body of a dead child in the Ravensbrück concentration camp

O Lord, remember not only the men and women of good will, but also those of ill will. But do not remember all the suffering they have inflicted on us; remember the fruits we have brought, thanks to this suffering – our comradeship, our loyalty, our courage, our generosity, the greatness of heart which has grown out of all this, and when they come to judgement let all the fruits which we have borne be their forgiveness.

Never be weary of doing good

John Wesley

You are never tired, O Lord, of doing us good; let us never be weary of doing you service. But as you have pleasure in the well-being of your servants, let us take pleasure in the service of our Lord, and abound in your work and in your love and praise ever-more.

Relieve the oppressed

Oliver Cromwell

Strengthen us, O God, to relieve the oppressed, to hear the groans of poor prisoners, to reform the abuses of all professions; that many be made not poor to make a few rich; for Jesus Christ's sake.

Teach me to serve you as you deserve

Ignatius Loyola

Dearest Lord, teach me to be generous;
teach me to serve you as you deserve;
to give and not to count the cost,
to fight and not to heed the wounds,
to toil and not to seek for rest,
to labour and not to seek reward,
except to know that I do your will.

Help me to spread your fragrance

J.H. Newman, used daily by the Missionaries of Charity

Dear Jesus, help me to spread your fragrance everywhere I go.

Flood my soul with your spirit and life.

Penetrate and possess my whole being so utterly that all my life may be only a radiance of yours.

Shine through me and be so in me that every soul we come into contact with may feel your presence in my soul.

Let them look up and see no longer me but only Jesus.

Deliver the oppressed

Clement of Rome
We beg you, Lord, to help and defend us.
Deliver the oppressed,
have compassion on the despised,
raise the fallen,
reveal yourself to the needy,
heal the sick,
bring back those who have strayed from you,
feed the hungry,
lift up the weak,
remove the prisoners' chains.
May every nation come to know that you are God alone,
that Jesus is your Son,
that we are your people, the sheep of your pasture.

To our fellow men – a heart of love

Augustine
Grant to us your servants:
to our God – a heart of flame;
to our fellow men – a heart of love;
to ourselves – a heart of steel.

Giving generously

The Treasury of Devotion
O Lord Jesus Christ, who though you were rich became poor, grant that all our desire for and covetousness of earthly possessions may die in us, and that the desire of heavenly things may live and grow in us. Keep us from all idle and vain expenses that we may always have enough to give to him who is in need, and that we may not give grudgingly or out of necessity, but cheerfully. Through your merits may we partake of the riches of your heavenly treasure.

The troubles and perils of people and nations

Anselm
We bring before you, O Lord,
the troubles and perils of people and nations,
the sighing of prisoners and captives,
the sorrows of the bereaved,
the necessities of strangers,
the helplessness of the weak,
the despondency of the weary,
the failing powers of the aged.
O Lord, draw near to each;
for the sake of Jesus Christ our Lord.

Love towards people is the bond of perfectness

Lord Shaftesbury
O God, the Father of the forsaken, who teaches us that love towards people is the bond of perfectness and the imitation of yourself: open our eyes and touch our hearts that we may see and do the things which belong to our peace.

Strengthen us in the work which we have undertaken; give us wisdom, perseverance, faith and zeal; and in your own time and according to your pleasure prosper our work; for the love of your Son Jesus Christ our Lord.

Sadness, Despair and Depression
Yet I will rejoice

Habakkuk 3:17–18 NRSV
Though the fig tree does not blossom,
    and no fruit is on the vines;
though the produce of the olive fails
    and the fields yield no food;
though the flock is cut off from the fold

and there is no herd in the stalls,
yet I will rejoice in the Lord;
    I will exult in the God of my salvation.

Do not hurt my flowers

George Herbert
Rain, do not hurt my flowers, but quickly spread
Your honey drops: press not to smell them here:
When they are ripe, their odour will ascend
And at your lodging will their thanks appear.

When comforts are declining

William Cowper
Sometimes a light surprises
    The Christian while he sings:
It is the Lord who rises
    With healing in his wings;
When comforts are declining,
    He grants the soul again
A season of clear shining
    To cheer it after rain.

All shall be well

Julian of Norwich
All shall be well, and all shall be well, and all manner of things shall be well.

Despair turns to hope

Anselm

Jesus, as a mother you gather your people to you:
You are gentle with us as a mother with her children;
Often you weep over our sins and our pride:
tenderly you draw us from hatred and judgement.
You comfort us in sorrow and bind up our wounds:
in sickness you nurse us,
and with pure milk you feed us.
Jesus, by your dying we are born to new life:
by your anguish and labour we come forth in joy.
Despair turns to hope through your sweet goodness:
through your gentleness we find comfort in fear.
Your warmth gives life to the dead:
your touch makes sinners righteous.
Lord Jesus, in your mercy heal us:
in your love and tenderness remake us.
In your compassion bring grace and forgiveness:
for the beauty of heaven may your love prepare us.

Deliver me from despair

Thomas Wilson

Grant, Lord God, that in the middle of all the discouragements, difficulties and dangers, distress and darkness of this mortal life, I may depend on your mercy, and on this build my hopes, as on a sure foundation. Let your infinite mercy in Christ Jesus deliver me from despair, both now and at the hour of death.

Mercy, Pity, Peace and Love

William Blake

To Mercy, Pity, Peace, and Love,
All pray in their distress,

And to these virtues of delight
Return their thankfulness.

For Mercy, Pity, Peace, and Love,
Is God our Father dear;
And Mercy, Pity, Peace, and Love,
Is Man, his child and care.

For Mercy has a human heart,
Pity, a human face;
And Love, the human form divine,
And Peace, the human dress.

Then every man, of every clime,
That prays in his distress,
Prays to the human form divine:
Love, Mercy, Pity, Peace.

My song is love unknown

Samuel Crossman

My song is love unknown,
My Saviour's love to me,
Love to the loveless shown,
That they might lovely be.
O, who am I,
That for my sake
My Lord should take
Frail flesh, and die?

He came from his blest throne,
Salvation to bestow:
But men made strange, and none
The longed-for Christ would know.
But O, my Friend,
My Friend indeed,

Who at my need
His life did spend!

Sometimes they strew his way,
and his sweet praises sing;
Resounding all the day
hosannas to their King;
Then 'Crucify!'
is all their breath,
And for his death
they thirst and cry.

Why, what hath my Lord done?
What makes this rage and spite?
He made the lame to run,
he gave the blind their sight.
Sweet injuries!
Yet they at these
Themselves displease,
and 'gainst him rise.

They rise, and needs will have
my dear Lord made away;
A murderer they save,
the Prince of Life they slay.
Yet cheerful he to suffering goes,
That he his foes
from thence might free.

Here might I stay and sing,
No story so divine;
Never was love, dear King,
Never was grief like thine!
This is my Friend,
In whose sweet praise
I all my days
Could gladly spend.

If we despair in ourselves

William Tyndale
He is our God, if we despair in ourselves and trust in him; and his
is the glory.

And sadness quits my soul

Horatius Bonar
Shine from the cross to me, then all is peace;
Shine from the throne, then all my troubles cease;
Speak but the word, and sadness quits my soul;
Touch but my hand with thine, and I am whole.

Bereavement and the Death of a Child
Enfolded in his love

Julian of Norwich, Revelations of Divine Love
In his love he clothes us, enfolds us and embraces us; that tender
love completely surrounds us, never to leave us.

The God of all consolation

2 Corinthians 1:3–4 NRSV
Blessed be the God and Father of our Lord Jesus Christ, the
Father of mercies and the God of all consolation, who consoles
us in all our affliction, so that we may be able to console those
who are in any affliction with the consolation with which we
ourselves are consoled by God.

We bless your name for all those who have entered into their rest

F.J.A. Hort

O Lord of all worlds, we bless your name for all those who have entered into their rest, and reached the promised land where you are seen face to face. Give us grace to follow in their footsteps, as they followed in the footsteps of your holy Son. Keep alive in us the memory of those dear to ourselves whom you have called to yourself; and grant that every remembrance which turns our hearts from things seen to things unseen may lead us always upwards to you, until we come to our eternal rest; through Jesus Christ our Lord.

I trace the rainbow through the rain

George Matheson

O Joy that seekest me through pain,
I cannot close my heart to thee;
I trace the rainbow through the rain,
And feel the promise is not vain,
That morn shall tearless be.

Grant that I may not sorrow as one without hope

E.W. Benson, on the death of his young son Martin

O God, to me who am left to mourn his departure, grant that I may not sorrow as one without hope for my beloved who sleeps in you; but, as always remembering his courage, and the love that united us on earth, I may begin again with new courage to serve you more fervently who are the only source of true love and true fortitude; that when I have passed a few more days in this valley of tears and this shadow of death, supported by your rod and staff, I may see him face to face, in those pastures and beside those waters of comfort where I believe he already walks with you. O Shepherd of the sheep, have pity on this darkened soul of mine.

You have reclaimed your lent jewels

Campbell Tait; five of his six children died of scarlet fever in one month, in 1856

O God, you have dealt very mysteriously with us. We have been passing through deep waters; our feet were well-nigh gone. But though you slay us, yet we will trust in you. ...You have reclaimed your lent jewels. Yet, O Lord, shall I not thank you now? I will thank you not only for the children you have left to us, but for those you have reclaimed. I thank you for the blessing of the last ten years, and for all the sweet memories of these lives. ... I thank you for the full assurance that each has gone to the arms of the Good Shepherd, whom each loved according to the capacity of her years. I thank you for the bright hopes of a happy reunion, when we shall meet to part no more. O Lord, for Jesus Christ's sake, comfort our desolate hearts.

Growing Old and Contemplating Death
My failing heart

Charles Wesley
In age and feebleness extreme,
Who shall a sinful worm redeem?
Jesus, my only hope thou art,
Strength of my failing flesh and heart;
Oh, could I catch a smile from thee,
And drop into eternity!

Glory to Thee, my God, this night

Thomas Ken
Forgive me, Lord, for thy dear Son,
The ill that I this day have done,
That with the world, myself, and thee
I, ere I sleep, at peace may be.

Teach me to live, that I may dread
The grave as little as my bed;
Teach me to die, that so I may
Rise glorious at the awful day.

O may my soul on thee repose,
And with sweet sleep mine eyelids close,
Sleep that may me more vigorous make
To serve my God when I awake.

When in the night I sleepless lie,
My soul with heavenly thoughts supply;
Let no ill dreams disturb my rest,
No powers of darkness me molest.

Die in Thy favour

William Laud
Grant, O Lord, that we may
live in Thy fear,
die in Thy favour,
rest in Thy peace,
rise in Thy power,
reign in Thy glory;
for Thine own beloved Son's sake,
Jesus Christ, our Lord.

Abide with me; fast falls the eventide

H.F. Lyte
Abide with me; fast falls the eventide;
The darkness deepens; Lord, with me abide!
When other helpers fail, and comforts flee,
Help of the helpless, O abide with me.

Swift to its close ebbs out life's little day;
Earth's joys grow dim, its glories pass away;
Change and decay in all around I see;
O thou who changest not, abide with me.

I need thy presence every passing hour;
What but thy grace can foil the tempter's power?
Who like thyself my guide and stay can be?
Through cloud and sunshine, O abide with me.

I fear no foe with thee at hand to bless;
Ills have no weight, and tears no bitterness.
Where is death's sting? where, grave, thy victory?
I triumph still, if thou abide with me.

Hold thou thy cross before my closing eyes;
Shine through the gloom, and point me to the skies:
Heaven's morning breaks, and earth's vain shadows flee;
In life, in death, O Lord, abide with me!

Evening is at hand

Lancelot Andrewes

O Lord, evening is at hand, furnish it with brightness. As day has its evening so also has life; the even of life is age, age has overtaken me, furnish it with brightness. Cast me not away in the time of age; forsake me not when my strength fails me. Do thou make, do thou bear, do thou carry and deliver me. Abide with me, Lord, for it is toward evening, and the day is far spent of this fretful life. Let thy strength be made perfect in my weakness.

This short life

Dr Johnson, written in his private register when he was 67 years old, on 25 July 1776

O God who has ordained that whatever is to be desired should be sought by labour, and who, by your blessing, brings honest labour to good effect, look with mercy on my studies and endeavours. Grant me, O Lord, to design only what is lawful and right; and afford me calmness of mind and steadiness of purpose, that I may so do your will in this short life, as to obtain happiness in the world to come, for the sake of Jesus Christ our Lord.

Grow old along with me!

Robert Browning

Grow old along with me!
The best is yet to be,
The last of life, for which the first was made:
Our times are in his hand
Who saith, 'A whole I planned,
Youth shows but half; trust God: see all, nor be afraid!'

Even to our old age

Augustine, as he contemplated old age

Lord, our God, we are in the shadow of your wings. Protect us and bear us up. You will care for us as if we were little children, even to our old age. When you are our strength we are strong, but when we are our own strength we are weak. Our good always lives in your presence, and we suffer when we turn our faces away from you. We now return to you, O Lord, that we may never turn away again.

Death will come one day to me

Latin, seventeenth-century, translated by H.W. Baker

Dying, let me still abide
Jesu, grant me this, I pray,
Ever in thy heart to stay;
Let me evermore abide
Hidden in thy wounded side.

If the evil one prepare,
Or the world, a tempting snare,
I am safe when I abide
In thy heart and wounded side.

If the flesh, more dangerous still,
Tempt my soul to deeds of ill,
Naught I fear when I abide
In thy heart and wounded side.

Death will come one day to me;
Jesu, cast me not from thee:
Dying let me still abide
In thy heart and wounded side.

In your love you have taken from me

Mechthild of Magdeburg
Lord, thank you that in your love you have taken from me all
earthly riches, and that you now clothe me and feed me
through the kindness of others. Lord, thank you that since you
have taken from me my sight, you serve me now with the eyes
of others.

Lord, thank you that since you have taken away the power of
my hands and my heart, you serve me through the hands and
hearts of others. Lord, I pray for them. Reward them with your

heavenly love, that they may faithfully serve and please you until they reach their happy end.

Death shall be no more

John Donne

Death be not proud, though some have callèd thee
Mighty and dreadful, for thou art not so;
For those whom thou thinkst thou dost overthrow
Die not, poor death, nor yet canst thou kill me;
From rest and sleep, which but thy pictures be,
Much pleasure, then from thee, much more must flow,
And soonest our best men with thee do go,
Rest of their bones, and soul's delivery.
Thou art slave to fate, chance, kings, and desperate men,
And dost with poison, war, and sickness dwell;
And poppy or charms can make us sleep as well
And better than thy stroke; why swellst thou then?
One short sleep past, we wake eternally,
And death shall be no more: death thou shalt die.

Facing Death
Many mansions

John 14:1–4 AV

Let not your heart be troubled: ye believe in God, believe also in me.

In my Father's house are many mansions: if it were not so, I would have told you. I go to prepare a place for you.

And if I go and prepare a place for you, I will come again, and receive you unto myself; that where I am, there ye may be also.

And whither I go ye know, and the way ye know.

When comes the hour of failing breath

Paul Eber, 1557, translated by Catherine Winkworth, 1858

Lord Jesus Christ, true Man and God
Who borest anguish, scorn, the rod,
And diedst at last upon the tree,
To bring thy Father's grace to me;
I pray thee, through that bitter woe,
Let me, a sinner, mercy know.

When comes the hour of failing breath,
And I must wrestle, Lord, with death,
Then come, Lord Jesus, come with speed,
And help me in my hour of need.
Lead me from this dark vale beneath,
And shorten then the pangs of death.

Joyful my resurrection be;
Thou in the judgement plead for me,
And hide my sins, Lord, from thy face,
And give me life, of thy dear grace.
I trust in Thee, O blessed Lord,
And claim the promise of thy Word.

Time

Inscription on clock in Chester Cathedral

When, as a child, I laughed and wept,
Time crept.
When, as a youth, I dreamed and talked,
Time walked.
When I became a full-grown man,
Time ran.
And later, as I older grew,
Time flew.
Soon I shall find, while travelling on,

Time gone.
Will Christ have saved my soul by then?
Amen.

I crave nothing for mine own merits

**Thomas Cranmer, his last words, before going to the stake,
21 March 1556**

O Father of heaven, O Son of God, Redeemer of the world, O
Holy Ghost, three persons and one God, have mercy upon me,
most wretched caitiff and miserable sinner. I have offended both
against heaven and earth more than my tongue can express.
Whither, then, may I go, or whither shall I flee? To heaven I may
be ashamed to lift up mine eyes, and in earth I find no place of
refuge or succour. To thee, therefore, O Lord, do I run; to thee do
I humble myself, saying, O Lord my God, my sins be great, but
yet have mercy upon me for thy great mercy. The great mystery
that God became man was not wrought for little or few offences.
Thou didst not give thy Son, O heavenly Father, unto death for
small sins only, but for all the greatest sins of the world, so that the
sinner return to thee with his whole heart, as I do at this present.
Wherefore have mercy on me, O God, whose property is always
to have mercy; have mercy upon me, O Lord, for thy great mercy.
I crave nothing for mine own merits, but for thy name's sake.

Lead, Kindly Light

J.H. Newman

Lead, Kindly Light, amid the encircling gloom,
  Lead Thou me on!
The night is dark, and I am far from home –
  Lead Thou me on!
Keep Thou my feet; I do not ask to see
The distant scene – one step enough for me.

I was not ever thus, nor pray'd that Thou
  Shouldst lead me on.
I loved to choose and see my path, but now
  Lead Thou me on!
I loved the garish day, and, spite of fears,
Pride ruled my will: remember not past years.

So long Thy power hath blest me, sure it still
  Will lead me on,
O'er moor and fen, o'er crag and torrent, till
  The night is gone;
And with the morn those angel faces smile
Which I have loved long since, and lost awhile.

From death to life

Meditations and Prayers, *compiled by John Cosin*
From death to life: from sorrow to joy: from a vale of misery to a paradise of mercy.

I know that my Redeemer liveth, and that I shall be raised again in the last day.

I shall walk before the Lord in the land of the living.

In thee, O Lord, have I trusted: let me never be confounded.

Into thy hands I commend my spirit: for thou has redeemed me, O Lord, thou God of truth.

Thou art my helper and Redeemer: make no long tarrying, O my God.

Come, Lord Jesu, come quickly.

Lord Jesus, receive my spirit.

The Lord receive my soul

William Laud, martyred on Tower Hill, 10 January 1645

O eternal God and merciful Father, look down upon me in mercy; in the riches and fullness of all Thy mercies, look down upon me: but not till Thou hast nailed my sins to the Cross of Christ, not till Thou has bathed me in the Blood of Christ, not till I have hid myself in the wounds of Christ, that so the punishment due unto my sins may pass over me. And since Thou art pleased to try me to the utmost, I humbly beseech Thee, give me now, in this great instant, full patience, proportionable comfort, and a heart ready to die for Thine honour, the King's happiness, and the Church's preservation.

I am coming, O Lord, as quickly as I can. I know I must pass through death before I can come to see Thee. But it is only the mere shadow of death; a little darkness upon nature. Thou, by Thy merits, hast broken through the jaws of death. The Lord receive my soul, and have mercy upon me, and bless this kingdom with peace and plenty, and with brotherly love and charity, that there may not be this effusion of Christian blood among them: for Jesus Christ's sake, if it be Thy will.

Lord, receive my soul.

And when we die

Reginald Heber
God that madest earth and heaven,
Darkness and light,
Who the day for toil hast given,
For rest the night;
Guard us waking, guard us sleeping,
And when we die:
May we in thy mighty keeping
All peaceful lie.

I am God's wheat

Ignatius of Antioch, prior to his martyrdom
Father, make us more like Jesus. Help us to bear difficulty, pain, disappointment and sorrow, knowing that in your perfect working and design you can use such bitter experiences to mould our characters and make us more like our Lord. We look with hope to the day when we will be completely like Christ, because we will see him as he is ...

I am God's wheat. May I be ground by the teeth of the wild beasts until I become the fine wheat bread that is Christ's. My passions are crucified, there is no heat in my flesh, a stream flows murmuring inside me; deep down in me it says: Come to the Father.

Our last awakening

John Donne, Progress of the Soul
Bring us, O Lord God, at our last awakening into the house and gate of heaven, to enter that gate and dwell in that house, where there shall be no darkness nor dazzling, but one equal light; no noise nor silence, but one equal music; no fears nor hopes, but one equal possession; no ends nor beginnings, but one equal eternity; in the habitations of thy glory and dominion, world without end.

My God shall raise me up, I trust

Sir Walter Raleigh, written on the fly-leaf of his Bible the night before he was executed at the Tower of London
Even such is time, that takes in trust
Our youth, our joys, our all we have,
And pays us but with earth and dust;
Who in the dark and silent grave,
When we have wandered all our ways
Shuts us the story of our days;

But from this earth, this grave, this dust,
My God shall raise me up, I trust.

Till in heaven we take our place

Charles Wesley
Finish, then, Thy new creation;
Pure and spotless let us be.
Let us see Thy great salvation
Perfectly restored in Thee;
Changed from glory into glory,
Till in heaven we take our place,
Till we cast our crowns before Thee,
Lost in wonder, love, and praise.

A firm hope

John Huss, as he lay chained in prison
O loving Christ, draw me, a weakling, after yourself; for if you do not draw me I cannot follow you. Give me a brave spirit that it may be ready alert. If the flesh is weak, may your grace go before me, come alongside me and follow me; for without you I cannot do anything, and especially, for your sake I cannot go to a cruel death. Grant me a ready spirit, a fearless heart, a right faith, a firm hope, and a perfect love, that for your sake I may lay down my life with patience and joy.

I praise you for all things

Polycarp
Polycarp, bishop of Smyrna and a disciple of the apostles, was burned at the stake in about the year 155. This is the prayer he prayed before he died.

Lord, almighty God, Father of your beloved and blessed Son Jesus Christ, through whom we have come to the knowledge of yourself, God of angels, of powers, of all creation, of all the race of saints who live in your sight, I bless you for judging me worthy of this day, this hour, so that in the company of the martyrs I may share the cup of Christ, your anointed one, and so rise again to eternal life in soul and body, immortal through the power of the Holy Spirit. May I be received among the martyrs in your presence today as a rich and pleasing sacrifice. God of truth, stranger to falsehood, you have prepared this and revealed it to me and now you have fulfilled your promise.

I praise you for all things, I bless you, I glorify you through the eternal priest of heaven, Jesus Christ, your beloved Son. Through him be glory to you, together with him and the Holy Spirit, now and forever. Amen.

Last Words of People About to Die

Joseph Addison
See in what peace a Christian can die.

Anne Askew, burned at the stake after torture on the rack, 16 July 1545, at the age of 25
I am not come hither to deny my Lord and Master.

Richard Baxter
I have pain (there is no arguing against sense); but I have peace, I have peace.

Thomas Becket
I am ready to die for my Lord, that in my blood the Church may obtain liberty and peace.

Henry Ward Beecher
Now comes the mystery.

Bernard of Clairvaux
I beg you, dearest brethren, love one another.

William Booth, end of his last speech
While women weep, as they do now, I'll fight; while men go to prison, in and out, in and out, as they do now, I'll fight; where there is a drunkard left, while there is a poor lost girl upon the streets, where there remains one dark soul without the light of God – I'll fight! I'll fight to the very end.

John Bradford, to fellow martyr John Leaf, at the stake, Smithfield, 1555
Be of good comfort, brother, for we shall have a merry supper with the Lord this night.

Elizabeth Barrett Browning, in reply to her husband who had asked how she felt
Beautiful.

Joseph Butler
Though I have endeavoured to avoid sin, and to please God to the utmost of my power, yet, from the consciousness of perpetual infirmities, I am still afraid to die. [His chaplain replied: 'My Lord, you have forgotten that Jesus Christ is a Saviour.'] True, but how shall I know that he is a saviour for me? ['My Lord,' answered the chaplain, 'it is written, "Him that cometh to me I will in no wise cast out".'] True, and I am surprised that, although I have read that Scripture a thousand times over, I have never felt its virtue till this moment; and now I die happy.

William Carey
When I am gone, speak less of Dr Carey and more of Dr Carey's Saviour.

Christ's seven 'last words'

Luke 23:34 AV
Father, forgive them, for they know not what they do.

Luke 23:43 AV
Today shalt thou be with me in paradise.

John 19:26 AV
Woman, behold thy Son.

Mark 15:34 AV
My God, My God, why hast thou forsaken me?

John 19:28 AV
I thirst.

John 19:30 AV
It is finished.

Luke 23:46 AV
Father, into thy hands I commend my spirit.

Oliver Cromwell
Lord, however Thou dispose of me, continue and go on to do good for them. Pardon Thy foolish people! Forgive their sins and do not forsake them, but love and bless them. Give them consistency of judgement, one heart, and mutual love; and go on to deliver them, and with the work of reformation; and make the name of Christ glorious in the world. Teach those who look too much on Thy instruments, to depend more upon Thyself... And pardon the folly of this short prayer. And give me rest for Jesus Christ's sake, to whom, with Thee and Thy Holy Spirit, be all honour and glory, now and forever! Amen.

Emily Dickinson
... the fog is rising.

Richard Grenville

Here die I, Richard Grenville, with a joyful and quiet mind, that I have ended my life as a true soldier ought to do that hath fought for his country, Queen, religion and honour. Whereby my soul most joyfully departeth out of this body, and shall always leave behind it an everlasting fame of a valiant and true soldier that hath done his duty as he was bound to do.

Matthew Henry

You have been used to take notice of the sayings of dying men. This is mine: that a life spent in the service of God, and in communion with him, is the most comfortable and pleasant life that anyone can live in this world.

John Hooper, written the night before his execution in 1555

Let nothing cause thy heart to fail;
Launch out thy boat, hoist up thy sail,
Put from the shore;
And be sure thou shalt attain
Unto the port that shall remain
For evermore.

John Huss, to his executioner

The meaning of Huss's name in Bohemian is 'goose'; Martin Luther, who came about a hundred years after him, had a swan for his arms.

You are now going to burn a goose, but in a century you will have a swan whom you can neither roast nor boil.

John Huss

O holy simplicity!

Adoniram Judson

I am not tired of my work, neither am I tired of the world; yet when Christ calls me home, I shall go with the gladness of a boy bounding away from school.

John Knox

Live in Christ, live in Christ, and the flesh need not fear death.

Hugh Latimer

Be of good comfort, Master Ridley, and play the man; we shall this day light such a candle, by God's grace, in England, as I trust shall never be put out ... Father of heaven, receive my soul!

William Law

Away with these filthy garments. I feel a sacred fire kindled in my soul, which will destroy everything contrary to itself, and burn as a flame of divine love to all eternity.

John Leland

I give my dying testimony to the truth of Christianity. The promises of the gospel are my support and consolation. They, alone, yield me satisfaction in a dying hour. I am not afraid to die. The gospel of Christ has raised me above the fear of death; for I know that my redeemer liveth.

Martyn Lloyd-Jones

On 1 March 1981, Dr David Martyn Lloyd-Jones died. He served as the pastor of Westminster Chapel in London from 1939 to 1968. He wrote these words on a scrap of paper a few days before his death, having lost the power of speech.

Do not pray for healing. Do not hold me back from the glory.

Martin Luther, repeated three times

God so loved the world that he gave his only begotten Son, that whosoever believeth in him should not perish but have everlasting life.

J. Gresham Machen

I'm so thankful for active obedience of Christ. No hope without it.

Robert Murray M'Cheyne, as he lay dying, aged 29

God gave me a message to deliver and a horse to ride. Alas, I have killed the horse and now I cannot deliver the message.

F.B. Meyer

You will tell the others I am going home a little sooner than I thought. Then tell them not to talk about the servant but to talk about the Saviour.

D.L. Moody

Earth is receding; heaven is approaching. This is my crowning day!

St Patrick

See now, I commend my soul to God for whom I am an ambassador because he chose me for this task, despite my obscurity, to be one of the least among his servants. This is my confession before I die.

Samuel Rutherford

If he should slay me ten thousand times, ten thousand times I'll trust. I feel, I feel, I believe in joy and rejoice; I feed on manna. O for arms to embrace him! O for a well-tuned harp!

Sir Walter Scott, from J.G. Lockhart, Life of Sir Walter Scott

Sir Walter Scott expressed the wish, as he lay dying, that I should read to him, and when I asked him from what book, he said, 'Need you ask? There is but one.' I chose the fourteenth chapter of St John's Gospel. Then Sir Walter Scott said, 'Well, this is great comfort.'

Philip Sidney

Love my memory; cherish my friends; but above all, govern your will and affection by the will and word of your Creator; in my beholding the end of this world, with all her vanities.

Charles Simeon

I wish to be alone, with my God, and to lie before him as a poor, wretched, hell-deserving sinner ... But I would also look to him as my all-forgiving God – and as my all-sufficient God and as my all-atoning God – and as my covenant-keeping God ... I would lie here to the last, at the foot of the cross, looking unto Jesus; and go as such into the presence of my God ... Jesus Christ is all in all for my soul, and now you must be all for my body. I cannot tell you any longer what I want. My principles were not founded on fancies or enthusiasm; there is a reality in them, and I find them sufficient to support me in death.

Stephen, Acts 7:59

And they stoned Stephen as he was calling on God and saying, 'Lord Jesus, receive my spirit'.

Hudson Taylor

I am so weak that I can hardly write, I cannot read my Bible, I cannot even pray, I can only lie still in God's arms like a little child, and trust.

Teresa of Avila *1515-82 - Spanish Carmelite Mystic.*

The hour I have long wished for is now come.

Augustus Toplady

The sky is clear; there is no cloud; come, Lord Jesus, come quickly.

Charles Wesley

I shall be satisfied with thy likeness – satisfied, satisfied.

John Wesley

The best of all is, God is with us. Farewell!

George Whitefield

I am tired in the Lord's work, but not tired of it.

Heaven

My life is hid in him that is my treasure

George Herbert, The Temple, Colossians 3:3
My *words and thoughts do both express this notion,*
That Life *hath with the sun a double motion.*
The first Is *straight, and our diurnal friend;*
The other Hid, *and doth obliquely bend.*
One life is wrapt In *flesh, and tends to earth:*
The other winds towards Him, *whose happy birth*
Taught me to live here so That *still one eye*
Should aim and shoot at that which Is *on high;*
Quitting with daily labour all My *pleasure,*
To gain at harvest an eternal Treasure.

PART FOUR

CHRISTIAN FESTIVALS AND THE CHRISTIAN YEAR

Sundays
Prayer for Sundays

Francis of Assisi, Prayer for Sundays and major feast days, to be said at nine o'clock in the morning (Terce)
Shout joyfully to God, all the earth,
sing praise to his name,
proclaim his glorious praise.

Say to God: How tremendous your deeds are!
On account of your great strength
your enemies woo your favour.

Let the whole earth worship you,
singing praises, singing praises to your name.

Come and listen,
all you who fear God,
while I tell you what great things
he has done for me.

To him I cried aloud,
high praise was on my tongue.

From his holy temple
he heard my voice,
my entreaty reached his ears.

Bless our God, you peoples,
loudly proclaim his praise.

In him will every race
in the world be blessed;
all nations will proclaim his glory.

Blessed be the Lord, the God of Israel,
who alone does wondrous deeds.

Blessed forever be his glorious name;
may the whole world be filled with his glory.
Amen. Amen.

The first day of the week

Lancelot Andrewes

O Lord Jesus Christ, who on the first day of the week rose again: Raise up our souls to serve the living God; and as you did also on this day send down on your apostles your most Holy Spirit, so take not the same Spirit from us, but grant that we may be daily renewed and plentifully enriched by his power; for your own mercy's sake, who lives and reigns with the Father and the Holy Spirit, ever one God, world without end.

Harvest
All good gifts around us

Matthias Claudius

We plough the fields and scatter
The good seed on the land.

But it is fed and watered
By God's almighty hand.
He sends the snow in winter,
The warmth to swell the grain,
The breezes and the sunshine,
And soft, refreshing rain:
All good gifts around us are sent from heaven above;
Then thank the Lord, O thank the Lord,
for all his love.

Advent
When your Son our Lord comes

Gelasian Sacramentary

We beseech you, O Lord, to purify our consciences by your daily visitation; that when your Son our Lord comes, he may find in us a mansion prepared for himself; through the same Jesus Christ our Lord.

Christmas
Be born in us today

Phillips Brooks

O holy Child of Bethlehem,
Descend to us, we pray;
Cast out our sin, and enter in:
Be born in us today.
We hear the Christmas angels
The great glad tidings tell:
O come to us, abide with us,
Our Lord Emmanuel.

Rightly to remember the birth of Jesus

R.L. Stevenson

O God, our loving Father, help us rightly to remember the birth
of Jesus, that we may share in the songs of the angels, the gladness
of the shepherds, and the worship of the wise men. May the
Christmas morning make us happy to be Thy children, and the
Christmas evening bring us to our beds with grateful thoughts,
forgiving and forgiven, for Jesus' sake.

Worship Christ the new-born King

James Montgomery

Angels, from the realms of glory,
Wing your flight o'er all the earth,
Ye who sang creation's story,
Now proclaim Messiah's birth;
Come and worship,
Worship Christ the new-born King.

Shepherds, in the field abiding,
Watching o'er your flocks by night,
God with man is now residing,
Yonder shines the infant-light;
Come and worship,
Worship Christ the new-born King.

Sages, leave your contemplations,
Brighter visions beam afar;
Seek the great Desire of nations;
Ye have seen His natal star;
Come and worship,
Worship Christ the new-born King.

Saints before the altar bending,
Watching long in hope and fear,

Suddenly the Lord, descending,
In His temple shall appear;
Come and worship,
Worship Christ the new-born King.

Sinners, wrung with true repentance,
Doom'd for guilt to endless pains,
Justice now revokes the sentence,
Mercy calls you, – break your chains;
Come and worship,
Worship Christ the new-born King.

Love all lovely, love divine

Christina Rossetti
Love came down at Christmas,
Love all lovely, love divine;
Love was born at Christmas,
Star and angels gave the sign.

Worship we the Godhead,
Love incarnate, love divine;
Worship we our Jesus:
But wherewith for sacred sign?

Love shall be our token,
Love shall be yours and love be mine,
Love to God and to all men,
Love for plea and gift and sign.

To take our nature upon him

English reformers, 1549
Almighty God, who hast given us thy only-begotten Son to take
our nature upon him, and as at this time to be born of a pure

Virgin: Grant that we, being regenerate and made thy children by adoption and grace, may daily be renewed by thy Holy Spirit; through the same our Lord Jesus Christ, who liveth and reigneth with thee and the same Spirit ever, one God, world without end. Amen.

Shall I be silent?

George Herbert

The shepherds sing; and shall I be silent?
My God, no hymn for thee?
My soul's a shepherd too; a flock it feeds
Of thoughts, and words and deeds.
The pasture is thy word: the streams thy grace
Enriching all the place.
Shepherd and flock shall sing, and all my powers
Out-sing the daylight hours.
Then we will chide the sun for letting night
Take up his place and right:
We sing one common Lord; wherefore he should
Himself the candle hold.
I will go searching, till I find a sun
Shall stay, till we have done;
A willing shiner, that shall shine as gladly,
As frost-nipt suns look sadly.
Then we will sing, and shine all our own day,
And one another pray:
His beams shall cheer my breast, and both so twine,
Till ev'n his beams sing, and my music shine.

*The yearly remembrance of the birth of your only
Son Jesus Christ*

Gelasian Sacramentary

O God, who makes us glad with the yearly remembrance of the birth of your only Son Jesus Christ: Grant that as we joyfully receive him for our Redeemer, so we may with sure confidence behold him when he comes to be our Judge; who lives and reigns with you and the Holy Spirit, ever one God, world without end.

In the bleak mid-winter

Christina Rossetti

*In the bleak mid-winter
    Frosty wind made moan,
Earth stood hard as iron,
    Water like a stone;
Snow had fallen, snow on snow,
    Snow on snow,
In the bleak mid-winter
    Long ago.*

*Our God, Heaven cannot hold Him,
    Nor earth sustain;
Heaven and earth shall flee away
    When He comes to reign:
In the bleak mid-winter
    A stable-place sufficed
The Lord God Almighty
    Jesus Christ.*

*Enough for Him whom cherubim
    Worship night and day,
A breastful of milk
    And a mangerful of hay;
Enough for Him whom angels*

Fall down before,
The ox and ass and camel
  Which adore.

Angels and archangels
  May have gathered there,
Cherubim and seraphim
  Throng'd the air,
But only His mother
  In her maiden bliss
Worshipped the Beloved
  With a kiss.

What can I give Him,
  Poor as I am?
If I were a shepherd
  I would bring a lamb,
If I were a wise man
  I would do my part –
Yet what I can I give Him,
  Give my heart.

Epiphany

Gloriously appeared to the shepherds

Mozarabic Liturgy

May our Lord Jesus Christ bless you, who of old on this day gloriously appeared to the shepherds in the manger. Amen.

May he himself protect and defend us in all things, who for us mercifully took upon himself our human infancy. Amen.

And may he, who is our Lord and Saviour, graciously keep us until eternity.

Lent
Keeping Lent

Robert Herrick

Is this a Fast, to keep
The larder lean?
And clean
From fat of veals and sheep?

Is it to quit the dish
Of flesh, yet still
To fill
The platter high with fish?

Is it to fast an hour,
Or ragg'd to go,
Or show
A down-cast look and sour?

No: 'tis a Fast to dole
Thy sheaf of wheat
And meat
Unto the hungry soul.

It is to fast from strife
And old debate,
And hate;
To circumcise thy life.

To show a heart grief-rent;
To starve thy sin,
Not bin;
And that's to keep thy Lent.

Easter (1) The Death of Christ
Palm Sunday

Henry Hart Milman
Ride on! ride on in majesty!
Hark! all the tribes 'Hosanna' cry:
O Saviour meek, pursue Thy road
With palms and scattered garments strowed.

Ride on! ride on in majesty!
In lowly pomp ride on to die:
O Christ, Thy triumphs now begin
O'er captive death and conquered sin.

Ride on! ride on in majesty!
The winged squadrons of the sky
Look down with sad and wondering eyes
To see the approaching sacrifice.

Ride on! ride on in majesty!
Thy last and fiercest strife is nigh;
The Father on His sapphire throne
Awaits His own anointed Son.

Ride on! ride on in majesty!
In lowly pomp ride on to die;
Bow thy meek head to mortal pain,
Then take, O God, Thy power and reign.

My God, my God, why have you forsaken me?

Psalm 22:1–11 NRSV
My God, my God, why have you forsaken me?
   Why are you so far from helping me, from the words of my groaning?
O my God, I cry by day, but you do not answer;
   and by night, but find no rest.

Yet you are holy,
enthroned on the praises of Israel.
In you our ancestors trusted;
they trusted, and you delivered them.
To you they cried, and were saved;
in you they trusted, and were not put to shame.
But I am a worm, and not human;
scorned by others, and despised by the people.
All who see me mock at me;
they make mouths at me, they shake their heads;
'Commit your cause to the Lord; let him deliver –
let him rescue the one in whom he delights!'
Yet it was you who took me from the womb;
you kept me safe on my mother's breast.
On you I was cast from my birth,
and since my mother bore me you have been my God.
Do not be far from me,
for trouble is near
and there is no one to help.

Good Friday 1613. Riding Westward

John Donne

Let man's Soul be a Sphere, and then, in this,
The intelligence that moves, devotion is,
And as the other Spheres, by being grown
Subject to foreign motions, lose their own,
And being by others hurried every day,
Scarce in a year their natural form obey:
Pleasure of business, so, our Souls admit
For their first mover, and are whirled by it.
Hence is 't, that I am carried towards the West
This day, when my Soul's form bends towards the East.
There I should see a Sun, by rising set,
And by that setting endless day beget;
But that Christ on this Cross, did rise and fall,

Sin had eternally benighted all.
Yet dare I almost be glad, I do not see
That spectacle of too much weight for me.
Who sees God's face, that is self life, must die;
What a death were it then to see God die?
It made his own Lieutenant Nature shrink,
It made his footstool crack, and the Sun wink.
Could I behold those hands which span the Poles,
And tune all spheres at once, pierc'd with those holes?
Could I behold that endless height which is
Zenith to us, and our Antipodes,
Humbled below us? or that blood which is
The seat of all our Souls, if not of his,
Made dirt of dust, or that flesh which was worn
By God, for his apparel, ragg'd, and torn?
If on these things I durst not look, durst I
Upon his miserable mother cast mine eye,
Who was God's partner here, and furnish'd thus
Half of that Sacrifice, which ransom'd us?
Though these things, as I ride, be from mine eye,
They are present yet unto my memory,
For that looks towards them; and thou look'st towards me,
O Saviour, as Thou hang'st upon the tree;
I turn my back to Thee, but to receive
Corrections, till Thy mercies bid Thee leave.
O think me worth Thine anger, punish me,
Burn off my rusts, and my deformity,
Restore Thine Image, so much, by Thy grace,
That Thou may'st know me, and I'll turn my face.

Hidden in thy wounded side

Latin, seventeenth-century, translated by H.W. Baker

Jesu, grant me this, I pray,
Ever in thy heart to stay;
Let me evermore abide
Hidden in thy wounded side.

If the evil one prepare,
Or the world, a tempting snare,
I am safe when I abide
In thy heart and wounded side.

If the flesh, more dangerous still,
Tempt my soul to deeds of ill,
Naught I fear when I abide
In thy heart and wounded side.

Death will come one day to me;
Jesu, cast me not from thee:
Dying let me still abide
In thy heart and wounded side.

Rock of ages

A.M. Toplady

Rock of ages, cleft for me,
Let me hide myself in Thee!
Let the water and the blood,
From Thy riven side which flowed,
Be of sin the double cure;
Cleanse me from its guilt and pow'r.

Not the labours of my hands
Can fulfil Thy law's demands:
Could my zeal no respite know,

Could my tears for ever flow,
All for sin could not atone:
Thou must save, and Thou alone!

Nothing in my hand I bring,
Simply to Thy Cross I cling;
Naked, come to Thee for dress;
Helpless, look to Thee for grace;
Foul, I to the fountain fly:
Wash me, Saviour, or I die!

While I draw this fleeting breath –
When my eye-strings break in death –
When I soar through tracts unknown –
See Thee on Thy judgement-throne –
Rock of ages, cleft for me,
Let me hide myself in Thee.

It is a thing most wonderful

W.W. How

It is a thing most wonderful,
Almost too wonderful to be,
That God's own Son should come from heaven,
And die to save a child like me.

And yet I know that it is true:
He chose a poor and humble lot,
And wept, and toiled, and mourned, and died
For love of those who loved him not.

But even could I see him die,
I could but see a little part
Of that great love, which, like a fire,
Is always burning in his heart.

It is most wonderful to know
His love for me so free and sure;
But 'tis more wonderful to see
My love for him so faint and poor.

And yet I want to love thee, Lord;
O light the flame within my heart,
And I will love thee more and more,
Until I see thee as thou art.

At the foot of thy Cross

Charles Kingsley

O Christ, give us patience and faith and hope as we kneel at the foot of thy Cross, and hold fast to it. Teach us by thy Cross that however ill the world may be, the Father so loved us that he spared not thee.

His hands and his side

Martin Luther

May our dear Lord Jesus Christ show you his hands and his side, and with his love put joy into your hearts, and may you behold and hear only him until you find your joy in him.

The Dream of the Rood

Author unknown

An eighth-century meditation on the death of Christ presented from the point of view of the rood (or cross) on which Christ was crucified.

Hear while I tell about the best of dreams
Which came to me the middle of one night
While humankind were sleeping in their beds.

It was as though I saw a wondrous tree
Towering in the sky suffused with light...

...the best
Of woods began to speak these words to me:
'It was long past – I still remember it –
That I was cut down at the copse's end,
Moved from my roots. Strong enemies there took me,
Told me to hold aloft their criminals,
Made me a spectacle. Men carried me
Upon their shoulders, set me on a hill,
A host of enemies there fastened me.
And then I saw the Lord of all mankind
Hasten with eager zeal that He might mount
Upon me. I durst not against God's word
Bend down or break, when I saw tremble all
The surface of the earth. Although I might
Have struck down all the foes, yet stood I fast.
Then the young hero (who was God almighty)
Got ready, resolute and strong in heart.
He climbed on to the lofty gallows-tree,
Bold in the sight of many watching men,
When he intended to redeem mankind.
I trembled as the warrior embraced me.
But still I dared not bend down to the earth,
Fall to the ground. Upright I had to stand.
A rood I was raised up; and I held high
The noble King, the Lord of heaven above.
I dared not stoop. They pierced me with dark nails;
The scars can still be clearly seen on me,
The open wounds of malice. Yet might I
Not harm them. They reviled us both together.
I was made wet all over with the blood
Which poured out from His side, after He had
Sent forth His spirit. And I underwent
Full many a dire experience on that hill.
I saw the God of hosts stretched grimly out.

Darkness covered the Ruler's corpse with clouds,
His shining beauty; the shadows passed across,
Black in the darkness. All creation wept,
Bewailed the King's death; Christ was on the cross.
And yet I saw men coming from afar,
Hastening to the Prince. I watched it all.'

When I survey the wondrous cross

Isaac Watts

When I survey the wondrous Cross,
   On which the Prince of glory died,
My richest gain I count but loss,
   And pour contempt on all my pride.

Forbid it, Lord, that I should boast
   Save in the death of Christ my God;
All the vain things that charm me most,
   I sacrifice them to his blood.

See from his head, his hands, his feet,
   Sorrow and love flow mingled down;
Did e'er such love and sorrow meet,
   Or thorns compose so rich a crown?

His dying crimson like a robe,
   Spreads o'er his body on the Tree;
Then am I dead to all the globe,
   And all the globe is dead to me.

Were the whole realm of nature mine,
   That were a present far too small;
Love so amazing, so divine,
   Demands my soul, my life, my all.

The first ten stations of the cross

The Treasury of Devotion
First station: Jesus is condemned to death
O innocent Jesus, who with wonderful submission wast for our sakes condemned to die. Grant that we may bear in mind that our sins were the false-witnesses; our blasphemies, backbitings, and evil speakings were the cause of thy accepting with gladness the sentence of the impious judge. O may this thought touch our hearts and make us hate those sins which caused thy death.

Second station: Jesus receives his cross
O blessed Jesus, grant us by virtue of thy cross and bitter passion, cheerfully to submit to and willingly to embrace all the trials and difficulties of this our earthly pilgrimage, and may we be always ready to take up our cross daily and follow thee.

Third station: Jesus falls under the weight of the cross
O Jesus, who for our sins didst bear the heavy burden of the cross and didst fall under its weight, may the thought of thy sufferings make us watchful against temptation, and do thou stretch out thy sacred hand to help us lest we fall into any grievous sin.

Fourth station: The cross is laid upon Simon of Cyrene
O Jesus! I thank thee, that thou has permitted me to suffer with thee, may it be my privilege to bear my cross, may I glory in nothing else; by it may the world be crucified unto me, and I unto the world, may I never shrink from suffering, but rather rejoice, if I be counted worthy to suffer for thy name's sake.

Fifth station: Jesus speaks to the women of Jerusalem
O Lord Jesus, we mourn and will mourn both for thee and for ourselves; for thy sufferings, and for our sins which caused them. O, teach us so to mourn, that we may be comforted, and escape those dreadful judgements prepared for all those who reject or neglect them.

Sixth station: Jesus is stripped of his garments
O Lord Jesus! Thou didst suffer shame for our most shameful deeds. Take from us, we beseech thee, all false shame, conceit, and pride, and make us so to humble ourselves in this life, that we may escape everlasting shame in the life to come.

Seventh station: Jesus is nailed to the cross
O Jesus! Crucified for me, subdue my heart with thy holy fear and love, and since my sins were the cruel nails that pierced thee, grant that in sorrow for my past life I may pierce and nail to thy cross all that offends thee.

Eighth station: Jesus hangs on the cross
O Jesus! we do devoutly embrace that honoured cross, where thou didst love us even unto death. In thy death is all our hope. Henceforth let us live only unto thee, so that whether we live or die we may be thine.

Ninth station: Jesus is taken down from the cross
O Lord Jesus, grant that we may never refuse that cross, which thou hast laid upon us: who willed not to be taken down from the cross, until thou hadst accomplished the work which thou camest to do.

Tenth station: Jesus is laid in the sepulchre
O Jesus, most compassionate Lord, we adore thee dead and enclosed in the holy sepulchre. We desire to enclose thee within our hearts, that, united to thee, we may rise to newness of life, and by the gift of final perseverance die in thy grace.

The wood of the cross

Ambrosian Manual
Lord Jesus Christ, who for the redemption of the world ascended the wood of the cross, and the whole world was turned into darkness, grant us always that light, both in body and soul, whereby we

may attain to everlasting life; who with the Father and the Holy
Spirit live and reign, one God, world without end.

Rex Tragicus, *or Christ Going to his Cross*

Robert Herrick
Put off thy robe of purple, then go on
To the sad place of execution:
Thine hour is come; and the tormentor stands
Ready, to pierce thy tender feet, and hands.
Long before this, the base, the dull, the rude,
Th' inconstant and unpurged multitude
Yawn for thy coming; some ere this time cry,
How he defers, how loath he is to die!
Amongst this scum, the soldier with his spear,
And that sour fellow, with his vinegar,
His sponge, and stick, do ask why thou dost stay?
So do the scurf and bran too: Go thy way,
Thy way, thou guiltless Man, and satisfy
By thine approach, each their beholding eye.
Not as a thief, shalt thou ascend the mount,
But like a person of some high account:
The cross shall be thy stage; and thou shalt there
The spacious field have for thy theatre.
Thou art that Roscius, and that marked-out man,
That must this day act the tragedian,
To wonder and affrightment: Thou art He,
Whom all the flux of nations comes to see;
Not those poor thieves that act their parts with Thee:
Those act without regard, when once a King,
And God, as thou art, comes to suffering.
No, no, this scene from thee takes life and sense,
And soul and spirit, plot and excellence.
Then begin, great King! ascend thy throne,
And thence proceed to act thy passion
To such a height, to such a period raised,

As hell, and earth, and heaven may stand amazed.
God, and good angels guide thee; and so bless
Thee in thy several parts of bitterness;
That those, who see thee nailed unto the tree,
May (though they scorn Thee) praise and pity Thee.
And we (Thy lovers) while we see Thee keep
The laws of action, will both sigh and weep;
And bring our spices, and embalm Thee dead;
That done, we'll see Thee sweetly buried.

The Sacrifice

George Herbert

O all ye, who pass by, whose eyes and mind
To worldly thing are sharp, but to be blind;
To me, who took eyes that I might you find:
Was ever grief like mine?...

Mine own Apostle, who the bag did bear,
Though he had all I had, did not forbear
To sell me also, and to put me there:
Was ever grief like mine?
For thirty pence he did my death devise,
Who at three hundred did the ointment prize,
Not half so sweet as my sweet sacrifice:
Was ever grief like mine?
Therefore my soul melts, and my heart's dear treasure
Drops blood (the only beads) my words to measure:
'O let this cup pass, if it be thy pleasure':
Was ever grief like mine?
These drops being temper'd with a sinner's tears,
A balsam are for both the Hemispheres,
Curing all wounds, but mine; all, but my fears:
Was ever grief like mine? ...
Arise, arise, they come! Look how they run!
Alas! what haste they make to be undone!

How with their lanterns do they seek the sun:
Was ever grief like mine?
With clubs and staves they seek me, as a thief,
Who am the way of truth, the true relief,
Most true to those who are my greatest grief:
Was ever grief like mine?
Judas, dost thou betray me with a kiss?
Canst thou find hell about my lips? and miss
Of life, just at the gates of life and bliss?
Was ever grief like mine?

See, they lay hold on me, not with the hands
Of faith, but fury; yet at their commands
I suffer binding, who have loosed their bands:
Was ever grief like mine?
All my disciples fly, fear puts a bar
Betwixt my friends and me. They leave the star,
That brought the wise men of the East from far:
Was ever grief like mine? ...
They bind, and lead me unto Herod: he
Sends me to Pilate. This makes them agree;
But yet friendship is my enmity:
Was ever grief like mine?
Herod and all his bands do set me light,
Who teach all hands to war, fingers to fight,
And only am the Lord of hosts and might:
Was ever grief like mine?
Herod in judgement sits, while I do stand;
Examines me with a censorious hand:
I him obey, who all things else command:
Was ever grief like mine?
The Jews accuse me with despitefulness;
And vying malice with my gentleness,
Pick quarrels with their only happiness:
Was ever grief like mine?
I answer nothing, but with patience prove
If stony hearts will melt with gentle love.

But who does hawk at eagles with a dove?
Was ever grief like mine? ...

Hark how they cry aloud still, 'Crucify:
It is not fit he live a day,' they cry,
Who cannot live less than eternally:
Was ever grief like mine?
Pilate a stranger holdeth off; but they,
Mine own dear people, cry, 'Away, away,'
With noises confused frighting the day:
Was ever grief like mine?
Yet still they shout, and cry, and stop their ears,
Putting my life among their sins and fears,
And therefore wish My blood on them and theirs:
Was ever grief like mine? ...
They choose a murderer, and all agree
In him to do themselves a courtesy;
For it was their own cause who killed me:
Was ever grief like mine?
And a seditious murderer he was:
But I the Prince of Peace; peace that doth pass
All understanding, more than heaven doth glass:
Was ever grief like mine? ...

Ah, how they scourge me! yet my tenderness
Doubles each lash: and yet their bitterness
Winds up my grief to a mysteriousness:
Was ever grief like mine?
They buffet me, and box me as they list,
Who grasp the earth and heaven with my fist,
And never yet, whom I would punish, miss'd:
Was ever grief like mine?
Behold, they spit on me in scornful wise;
Who with my spittle gave the blind man eyes,
Leaving his blindness to mine enemies:
Was ever grief like mine?
My face they cover, though it be divine.

As Moses' face was veiled, so is mine,
Lest on their double-dark souls either shine:
Was ever grief like mine?
Servants and abjects flout me; they are witty:
'Now prophesy who strikes thee,' is their ditty.
So they in me deny themselves all pity:
Was ever grief like mine?
And now I am deliver'd unto death,
Which each one calls for so with utmost breath,
That he before me well-nigh suffereth:
Was ever grief like mine?
Weep not, dear friends, since I for both have wept,
When all my tears were blood, the while you slept:
Your tears your own fortunes should be kept:
Was ever grief like mine?
The soldiers lead me to the common hall;
There they deride me, they abuse me all:
Yet for twelve heavenly legions I could call:
Was ever grief like mine?
Then in the scarlet robe they me array;
Which shows my blood to be the only way,
And cordial left to repair man's decay:
Was ever grief like mine?
Then on my head a crown of thorns I wear;
For these are all the grapes Sion doth bear,
Though I my vine planted and water'd there:
Was ever grief like mine?
So sits the earth's great curse in Adam's fall
Upon my head; so I remove it all
From th' earth unto my brows, and bear the thrall:
Was ever grief like mine?
Then with the reed they gave to me before,
They strike my head, the rock from whence all store
Of heavenly blessings issue evermore:
Was ever grief like mine?
They bow their knees to me, and cry, 'Hail, King,'
Whatever scoffs or scornfulness can bring,

I am the floor, the sink, where they it fling:
Was ever grief like mine?
Yet since man's sceptres are as frail as reeds,
And thorny all their crowns, bloody their weeds;
I, who am Truth, turn into truth their deeds:
Was ever grief like mine?
The soldiers also spit upon that face
Which angels did desire to have the grace,
And Prophets once to see, but found no place:
Was ever grief like mine?
Thus trimmed, forth they bring me to the rout,
Who 'Crucify him,' cry with one strong shout.
God holds his peace at man, and man cries out:
Was ever grief like mine?
They lead me in once more, and putting then
Mine own clothes on, they lead me out again.
Whom devils fly, thus is he toss'd of men:
Was ever grief like mine?
And now weary of sport, glad to engross
All spite in one, counting my life their loss,
They carried me to my most bitter cross:
Was ever grief like mine?
My cross I bear myself, until I faint:
Then Simon bears it for me by constraint,
The decreed burden of each mortal Saint:
Was ever grief like mine?
'O all ye who pass by, behold and see':
Man stole the fruit, but I must climb the tree;
The tree of life to all, but only me:
Was ever grief like mine?
Lo, here I hang, charged with a world of sin,
The greater world o' the two; for that came in
By words, but this by sorrow I must win:
Was ever grief like mine?
Such sorrow, as if sinful man could feel,
Or feel his part, he would not cease to kneel,
Till all were melted, though he were all steel:

Was ever grief like mine?
But, 'O my God, my God!' why leav'st thou me,
The Son, in whom thou dost delight to be?
'My God, my God'
Never was grief like mine?

Shame tears my soul, my body many a wound;
Sharp nails pierce this, but sharper that confound;
Reproaches, which are free, while I am bound:
Was ever grief like mine?
Now heal thyself, Physician; now come down.
Alas! I did so, when I left my crown
And Father's smile for you, to feel his frown:
Was ever grief like mine?
In healing not myself, there doth consist
All that salvation, which ye now resist;
Your safety in my sickness doth subsist:
Was ever grief like mine?
Betwixt two thieves I spend my utmost breath,
As he that for some robbery suffereth.
Alas! what have I stolen from you? death:
Was ever grief like mine?
A king my title is, prefix'd on high;
Yet by my subjects I'm condemn'd to die
A servile death in servile company:
Was ever grief like mine?
They gave me vinegar mingled with gall,
But more with malice: yet, when they did call,
With Manna, Angels' food, I fed them all:
Was ever grief like mine?
They part my garments, and by lot dispose
My coat, the type of love, which once cured those
Who sought for help, never malicious foes:
Was ever grief like mine?
Nay, after death their spite shall farther go;
For they will pierce my side, I full well know;
That as sin came, so Sacraments might flow:

Was ever grief like mine?
But now I die; now all is finished.
My woe, man's weal: and now I bow my head:
Only let others say, when I am dead,
Never was grief like mine.

Easter (2) The Resurrection of Christ
Easter Wings

George Herbert, The Temple

Lord, who createdst man in wealth and store,
Though foolishly he lost the same,
Decaying more and more,
Till he became
Most poor:
With thee
O let me rise
As larks, harmoniously,
And sing this day thy victories:
Then shall the fall further the flight in me.
My tender age in sorrow did begin:
And still with sickness and shame
Thou did'st so punish sin,
That I became
Most thin
With thee
Let me combine,
And feel this day the victory,
For, if I imp my wing on thine,
Affliction shall advance the flight in me.

Easter II

George Herbert, The Temple

I got me flowers to strew thy way;
I got me boughs off many a tree:
but thou wast up by break of day,
And bright thy sweets along with thee.

The Sun arising in the East,
Though he give light, and th' East perfume;
If they should offer to contest
With thy arising, they presume.

Can there be any day but this,
Though many suns to shine endeavour?
We count three hundred, but we miss:
There is but one, and that one ever.

My dancing day

Author unknown, fifteenth-century

Tomorrow shall be my dancing day:
I would my true love did so chance
to see the legend of my play,
To call my true love to my dance:

Refrain
Sing O my love, O my love, my love, my love;
This have I done for my true love.

Then was I born of a virgin pure,
Of here I took fleshly substance;
Thus was I knit to man's nature,
To call my true love to my dance:

Refrain

In a manger laid and wrapped I was,
So very poor, this was my chance,
Betwixt an ox and a silly poor ass,
To call my true love to my dance:

Refrain

Then afterwards baptized I was;
The Holy Ghost on me did glance,
My Father's voice heard from above,
To call my true love to my dance:

Refrain

Into the desert I was led,
Where I fasted without substance;
The devil bade me make stones my bread,
To call my true love to my dance:

Refrain

The Jews on me they made great suit,
And with me made great variance,
Because they loved darkness rather than light,
To call my true love to my dance:

Refrain

For thirty pence Judas me sold,
His covetousness for to advance;
'Mark whom I kiss, the same do hold,'
The same is he shall lead the dance.

Refrain

Before Pilate the Jews me brought,
Where Barabbas had deliverance;
They scourged me and set me at nought,
Judged me to die to lead the dance:

Refrain

Then on the cross hanged I was,
Where a spear to my heart did glance;
There issued forth both water and blood,
To call my true love to my dance:

Refrain

Then down to hell I took my way
For my true love's deliverance,
And rose again on the third day,
Up to my true love and the dance:

Refrain

Then up to heaven I did ascend,
Where now I dwell in sure substance,
On the right hand of God, that man
May come unto the general dance:

Refrain

Christ has burst the gates of hell

Charles Wesley
Love's redeeming work is done;
Fought the fight, the battle won:
Lo, our Sun's eclipse is o'er!
Lo, he sets in blood no more.

Vain the stone, the watch, the seal,
Christ has burst the gates of hell;
Death in vain forbids his rise;
Christ has opened Paradise.

Lives again our glorious King;
Where, O death, is now thy sting?
Dying once, he all doth save;
Where thy victory, O grave?

May live for ever in felicity

Edmund Spenser
Most glorious Lord of Life! that on this day
Didst make thy triumph over death and sin;
And, having harrowed hell, didst bring away
Captivity, thence captive, us to win:
This joyous day, dear Lord, with joy begin;
And grant that we, for whom thou didest die,
Being with thy dear blood clean washed from sin,
May live for ever in felicity.
And that thy love, we weighing worthily,
May likewise love thee for the same again;
And for thy sake, that all like dear didst buy,
With love may one another entertain!
    So let us love, dear Lord, like as we ought.
    – Love is the lesson which the Lord us taught.

Jesus Christ is risen today, Alleluya!

'Lyra Davidica', 1708, translated from a fourteenth-century manuscript
Jesus Christ is risen today, Alleluya!
Our triumphant holy day, Alleluya!

Who did once, upon the Cross, Alleluya!
Suffer to redeem our loss. Alleluya!

Hymns of praise then let us sing, Alleluya!
Unto Christ, our heavenly King, Alleluya!
Who endured the Cross and grave, Alleluya!
Sinners to redeem and save. Alleluya!

But the pains that he endured, Alleluya!
Our salvation have procured; Alleluya!
Now above the sky he's King, Alleluya!
Where the angels ever sing. Alleluya!

The joyful resurrection of the just

Martin Luther

Almighty God, who through the death of your Son has destroyed
sin and death, and by his resurrection has restored innocence and
everlasting life, that we may be delivered from the dominion of
the devil, and our mortal bodies raised up from the dead: Grant
that we may confidently and whole-heartedly believe this, and,
finally, with your saints, share in the joyful resurrection of the just;
through the same Jesus Christ, your Son, our Lord.

A Better Resurrection

Christina Rossetti

I have no wit, no words, no tears;
My heart within me like a stone
Is numbed too much for hopes or fears;
Look right, look left, I dwell alone;
I lift mine eyes, but dimmed with grief
No everlasting hills I see;
My life is in the falling leaf:
O Jesus, quicken me.

My life is like a faded leaf,
My harvest dwindled to a husk;
Truly my life is void and brief
And tedious in the barren dusk;
My life is like a frozen thing,
No bud nor greenness can I see:
Yet rise it shall — the sap of Spring;
O Jesus, rise in me.

My life is like a broken bowl,
A broken bowl that cannot hold
One drop of water for my soul
Or cordial in the searching cold;
Cast in the fire the perished thing,
Melt and remould it, till it be
A royal cup for Him my King:
O Jesus, drink of me.

Ascension
Into whose gracious presence we ascend

Leonine Sacramentary
Almighty and merciful God, into whose gracious presence we ascend, not by the frailty of the flesh but by the activity of the soul: Make us always by your inspiration to seek after the courts of the heavenly city, where our Saviour Christ has ascended, and by your mercy confidently to enter them, both now and hereafter; through the same Jesus Christ our Lord.

Pentecost
By his gracious in-dwelling

The Treasury of Devotion
Grant, we beseech thee, almighty and merciful God, that the Holy Ghost may come upon us, and by his gracious in-dwelling, may

make us a temple of his glory; through Jesus Christ our Lord.
Amen.

Sanctify us with your Holy Spirit

Philipp Melanchthon

Almighty God, eternal Father of our Lord Jesus Christ, creator of
heaven and earth and mankind, one with your Son and the Holy
Spirit, have mercy on us. Justify us through your Son, Jesus Christ,
and sanctify us with your Holy Spirit. Establish, guard and guide
your church, O God.

Veni, creator Spiritus

Translated by John Cosin

Come, Holy Ghost, our souls inspire,
And lighten with celestial fire;
Thou the anointing Spirit art,
Who dost thy sevenfold gifts impart:
Thy blessed unction from above
Is comfort, life, and fire of love;
Enable with perpetual light
The dullness of our blinded sight:
Anoint and cheer our soiled face
With the abundance of thy grace:
Keep far our foes, give peace at home;
Where thou art guide no ill can come.

Teach us to know the Father, Son,
And thee, of Both, to be but One;
That through the ages all along
This may be our endless song,

Praise to thy eternal merit,
Father, Son, and Holy Spirit. Amen

Two dwellings

Izaak Walton

I have heard a grave divine say, that God has two dwellings, one in heaven, and the other in the meek and thankful heart.

Trinity

Father of Heaven, The Son, The Holy Ghost

John Donne, from 'A Litanie'

The Father

> Father of Heaven, and Him, by whom
> It, and us for it, and all else for us
> Thou mad'st, and govern'st ever, come
> And re-create me, now grown ruinous:
> My heart is by dejection, clay,
> And by self-murder, red.
> From this red earth, O Father, purge away
> All vicious tinctures, that new fashionèd
> I may rise up from death, before I'm dead.

The Son

> O Son of God, who seeing two things,
> Sin and death, crept in, which were never made,
> By bearing one, tried'st with what stings
> The other could Thine heritage invade;
> O be Thou nail'd unto my heart,
> And crucified again.
> Part not from it, though it from Thee would part,
> But let it be, by applying so Thy pain,
> Drown'd in Thy blood, and in Thy passion slain.

The Holy Ghost

> O Holy Ghost, whose temple I
> Am, but of mud walls, and condensèd dust,

And being sacrilegiously
Half wasted with youth's fires, of pride and lust,
Must with new storms be weather-beat;
Double in my heart Thy flame,
Which let devout sad tears intend; and let
(Though this glass lanthorn, flesh, do suffer main)
Fire, Sacrifice, Priest, Altar be the same.

Bless, guard, enlighten me

Book of Cerne

God the Father bless me, Christ guard me, the Holy Spirit enlighten me, all the days of my life! The Lord be the defender and guardian of my soul and my body, now and always, world without end. Amen.

The right hand of the Lord preserve me always to old age!
The grace of Christ perpetually defend me from the enemy!
Direct, Lord, my heart into the way of peace.
Lord God, deliver and help me.

The Return of Christ
An overriding influence

Lord Shaftesbury

I do not think that in the last forty years I have lived one conscious hour that was not influenced by the thought of our Lord's return.

Suddenly return

Charles Wesley

Come, Almighty to deliver,
Let us all Thy life receive;
Suddenly return and never,

Never more Thy temples leave.
Thee we would be always blessing,
Serve Thee as Thy hosts above,
Pray and praise Thee without ceasing,
Glory in Thy perfect love.

INDEX OF SOURCES

Addison, Joseph, 1672–1719, English essayist and poet   199
Alcuin, c. 737–804, English scholar and theologian   99, 156
Ambrosian Manual   227
Andrewes, Lancelot, 1555–1626, Bishop of Chichester and then
    Winchester; one of the translators of the Authorized Version
    of the Bible   10, 102, 133, 189, 210
Anselm, 1033–1109, Archbishop of Canterbury   139, 143, 173,
    180, 182
Askew, Anne, 1520–45, martyr   199
Aquinas, Thomas, 1225–74, Italian Dominican monk, theologian
    and philosopher   7, 103, 108, 133
Arnold, Thomas, 1795–1842, Headmaster of Rugby School
    171
Astley, General Lord Jacob, 1579–1652, soldier   170
Augustine, 354–430, Bishop of Hippo in North Africa, very
    influential theologian   7, 10, 12, 51, 54, 65, 84, 113, 121, 168,
    179, 190
Augustine's Manual, fifth century   176
Austen, Jane, 1775–1817, English novelist   96
Aylward, Gladys, 1902–70, missionary to China   11

Baker, Henry Williams, 1821–77, hymn writer and editor of
    Hymns Ancient and Modern   191, 221
Barclay, William, 1907–78, New Testament scholar   9, 11
Basil the Great, c. 329–79, Bishop of Caesarea, theologian   114,
    168

Baxter, Richard, 1615–91, English Puritan minister and religious
   writer   86, 98, 174, 199
Becket, Thomas, 1118–70, Archbishop of Canterbury   199
Becon, Thomas, 1512–67, English Protestant divine   136
Beecher, Henry Ward, 1813–87, US preacher and journalist
   199
Benson, Edward White, 1829–96, Archbishop of Canterbury
   186
Bernard of Clairvaux, 1090–1153, Cistercian monk and abbot
   7, 138, 200
Beveridge, William, 1637–1708, Bishop of St Asaph   66
Blake, William, 1757–1827, poet and painter   182
Bode, John Ernest, 1816–74, hymn writer   88
Bonar, Horatius, 1808–82, hymn writer   108, 152, 165, 185
Boniface c. 680–c. 754, English missionary to Germany   175
Book of Cerne, a collection of hymns and prayers from Mercia,
   ninth century   244
Book of Hours, 1514   141
Book of Hours, 1864   136
Booth, William, 1829–1912, founder of the Salvation Army
   200
Bradford, John, 1510–55, martyred at Smithfield   200
Brady, Nicholas, 1639–1726, hymn writer   134, 164
Breton fisherman's prayer   161
Brontë, Anne, 1820–49, English novelist   76
Brooks, Phillips, 1835–93, Bishop of Massachusetts   170, 211
Browning, Elizabeth Barrett, 1806–61, English poet   200
Browning, Robert, 1812–89, English poet   147, 190
Bunyan, John, 1628–88, English preacher and author of The
   Pilgrim's Progress   63, 99
Butler, Joseph, 1692–1752, English royal chaplain and Bishop of
   Durham   200
Byrom, John, 1691–1763, English poet and hymn writer   52

Calvin, John, 1509–64, leading Reformation theologian   9, 65,
   109
Carey, William, English Baptist missionary to India   200

Caswell, Edward, 1814–78, hymn writer   138

Catherine of Siena, 1347–80, sister of the Dominican order   6, 51

Caussade, Jean-Pierre de, 1675–1751, French Jesuit writer and travelling preacher   8

Chalmers, Thomas, 1780–1847, Scottish divine   140

Charles I, 1600–49, King of England   10

Chester Cathedral   193

Chrysostom, John, c. 347–407, Bishop of Constantinople   9, 64, 127, 138

Clare College, Cambridge   141

Claudius, Matthias, 1740–1815, German poet   210

Clement XI, 1649–1721, pope 1700–21   93

Clement of Alexandria, c. 150–c. 215, Christian philosopher   126

Clement of Rome, c. 30–c. 95, reckoned to be the fourth Bishop (pope) of Rome   88, 179

Coleridge, Samuel Taylor, 1772–1834, English Romantic poet   153

Columba, 521–597, Irish missionary   63, 151

Companion or Spiritual Guide at the Altar, author unknown, 1783   106

Cosin, John, 1594–1672, Bishop of Durham   97, 116, 195, 242

Coventry Cathedral   94

Coverdale, Miles, 1488–1568, English Bible translator and Bishop of Exeter   137

Cowper, William, 1731–1800, English poet   103, 107, 158, 181

Cranmer, Thomas, 1489–1556, Archbishop of Canterbury, main compiler of *Book of Common Prayer*   105, 194

Cromwell, Oliver, 1599–1658, English revolutionary soldier and statesman   178, 201

Crossman, Samuel, c. 1624–83, Prebendary of Bristol Cathedral   183

Dickinson, Emily, 1830–1886, US poet   201

Doddridge, Philip, 1702–51, British nonconformist minister and hymn writer   89

Donne, John, 1572–1631, English poet and Dean of St Paul's
    Cathedral, London   11, 76, 82, 138, 192, 197, 219, 243
Drake, Sir Francis, c. 1540–96, greatest seaman of Elizabethan
    England   99
Dream of the Rood, The, author unknown, eighth century   223

Eber, Paul, sixteenth-century reformer   193
Elizabeth I, 1533–1603, Queen of England   105
Elliott, Charlotte, 1789–1871, hymn writer   85
Ephraem, c. 306–96, writer of the Syrian church   112
Erasmus, Desiderius, 1466–1536, Dutch humanist scholar
    who prepared an accurate edition of the Greek New
    Testament   83, 138

Fénelon, François, 1651–1715, French archbishop   11, 24
Fletcher, Phineas, 1582–1650, English poet   77
Fox, George, 1624–91, founder of the Religious Society of
    Friends (Quakers)   176
Francis de Sales, 1567–1622, Bishop of Geneva   7, 8, 66, 92, 120,
    126
Francis of Assisi, c. 1181–1226, Italian founder of the Franciscan
    order of friars   10, 57, 60, 150, 175, 209
Frankfurt prayer, author unknown, sixteenth century   120
Fuller, Thomas, 1608–61, English clergyman and popular
    historian   136

Gaelic prayers   135, 152
Gallican Sacramentary, author unknown, fifth to ninth centuries
    88, 95, 142
Gelasian Sacramentary, fifth century   173, 211, 215
Gertrude of Thüringen, known as Gertrude the Great,
    1256–1302, German mystic   91
Grenville, Richard, 1541–91, English naval commander   202
Gurnall, William, 1616–79, English Puritan minister   63

Hall, Joseph, 1574–1656, Bishop of Exeter   62, 71, 72
Hamilton, Robert, 1511–71, Archbishop   82

Hart, Joseph, 1712–68, independent minister and hymn writer
151

Hatch, Edwin, 1835–89, Reader in Ecclesiastical History at
Oxford 118

Havergal, Frances Ridley, 1836–70, poet and hymn writer 91

Heber, Reginald, 1783–1826, Bishop of Calcutta, poet and hymn
writer 196

Hebridean chant, traditional 157

Henry, Matthew, 1662–1714, nonconformist Bible
commentator 202

Herbert, George, 1593–1633, clergyman and poet 52, 63, 81,
98, 111, 124, 163, 170, 181, 206, 214, 229, 235, 236

Herrick, Robert, 1591–1679, poet 86, 217, 228

Homilies, apocryphal writings attributed to Clement, Bishop of
Rome towards the end of the first century 66

Hooper, John, ?–1555, Bishop of Gloucester and Worcester,
martyr 202

Hopkins, Gerard Manley, 1844–89, Jesuit priest 147

Hort, F.J.A., 1828–92, biblical scholar 186

How, William Walsham, 1823–97, first Bishop of Wakefield,
hymn writer 222

Huss, John, c. 1369–1415, Bohemian theologian, martyr 198,
202

Ignatius, Bishop of Antioch, martyred in c. 107 96, 197

Irish prayers, traditional 132

James I, 1566–1625, King of Great Britain 73

Jerome, c. 342–420, biblical scholar and Bible translator 91

John of the Cross, 1542–91, mystic and joint founder of the
Discalced Carmelites 117

John XXIII, 1881–1963, pope 1958–63 7

Johnson, Dr Samuel, 1709–1784, English writer and
lexicographer 102, 138, 190

Judson, Adoniram, 1788–1850, US missionary in Burma 202

Julian of Norwich, c. 1342–1413, English anchoress of Norwich
6, 122, 181, 185

Keble, John, 1792–1866, leader of the Oxford Movement   128, 142

Kempe, Margery, c. 1373–c. 1440, English mystic   159

Kempis, Thomas à, 1379–1471, Augustinian monk and reputed author of *Imitation of Christ*   7, 78, 155, 166, 169

Ken, Thomas, 1637–1711, Bishop of Bath and Wells   109, 129, 131, 157, 187

Kethe, William, d. 1593, hymn writer   55

Kierkegaard, Søren, 1813–55, attributed as founder of existentialist philosophy   120, 153, 159, 168

King's College, Cambridge   155

Kingsley, Charles, 1819–75, English clergyman, social reformer whose novels include *The Water Babies*   141, 149, 223

Knox, John, c. 1513–72, Chaplain to Edward VI of England, main compiler of the *Scottish Prayer Book*   156, 169, 203

Langland, William, c. 1332–c. 1400, English poet   59

Latimer, Hugh, 1485?–1555, Bishop of Worcester, martyr   203

Laud, William, 1573–1645, Archbishop of Canterbury   125, 188, 196

Law, William, 1686–1761, spiritual writer   83, 161, 203

Lawrence, Brother, 1605–91, French Carmelite lay brother   10, 58

Leland, John, 1506–52, English antiquary   203

Leonine Sacramentary, texts for the liturgy, associated with Leo I, pope 440–461   96, 169, 241

Lewis, Clive Staples, 1898–1963, English literary critic and writer of popular Christian apologetics   6

Lincoln, Abraham, 1809–65, President of USA   10

Liturgy of St Dionysius, third century   125

Liturgy of St James   122

Livingstone, David, 1813–73, Scottish medical missionary and explorer in Africa   155, 174

Lloyd-Jones, D. Martyn, 1899–1981, Welsh nonconformist minister   203

Loyola, Ignatius, 1491 or 1495–1556, founded the Jesuit order   178

Luther, Martin, 1483–1546, German monk and theologian who led the Protestant Reformation   84, 107, 108, 117, 133, 174, 203, 223, 240

Lutheran Manual of Prayer   132

Lyra Davidica, 1708   239

Lyte, Henry Francis, 1793–1847, Anglican clergyman, perpetual curate of Lower Brixham, Devon, hymn writer   123, 188

Machen, J. Gresham, 1881–1937, last major advocate of the Princeton theology   203

Margaret of Scotland, St, c.1045–93, wife of Michael III Canmore, King of Scotland, promoted reform of the church   6

Martyn, Henry, 1781–1812, scholar and pioneer missionary to India and Persia   92, 153

Matheson, George, 1842–1906, blind Scottish minister   53, 186

Mechthild of Magdeburg, 1210–97, medieval mystic   191

Melanchthon, Philipp, 1497–1560, German reformer and friend of Martin Luther   134, 242

Meyer, F.B., 1847–1929, English Baptist minister   204

Michelangelo, 1475–1564, Italian painter, artist, sculptor and inventor   10

Milman, Henry Hart, 1791–1868, hymn writer   218

Milton, John, 1608–1674, English poet   158

Montgomery, James, 1771–1854, hymn writer   59, 212

Moody, Dwight Lyman, 1837–99, American evangelist   177, 204

More, Thomas, 1478–1535, Lord Chancellor of England   12

Mozarabic Liturgy, the national liturgy of the Spanish Church until the eleventh century   158, 216

My dancing day, author unknown, fifteenth century   236

M'Cheyne, Robert Murray   64, 204

Nelson, Robert, eighteenth-century early Methodist field preacher   72

New England sampler, sixteenth and seventeenth century   134

Newman, John Henry, 1801–90, leader of the Anglican Oxford
    Movement   8, 9, 56, 132, 178, 194
Newton, John, 1725–1807, Anglican clergyman and hymn writer
    80, 104, 117, 141, 164
Nicholas of Flue, 1417–87, hermit   104
Niebuhr, Reinhold, 1892–1971, American theologian   140

Paget, Francis, 1851–1911, Bishop of Oxford   167
Paterson, Alexander, 1884–1947, prison reformer   176
Penn, William, 1644–1718, English Quaker, founder of
    Pennsylvania   11
Patrick, c. 385–461, English missionary to Ireland   81, 113, 160,
    204
Pierpoint, Folliott Sandford, 1835–1917, hymn writer   150
Polycarp, c. 69–c. 155, Bishop of Smyrna, knew the apostle John,
    burnt to death for his faith   198
Pusey, Edward Bouverie, 1800–82, Tractarian leader   3, 61, 135,
    163

Raleigh, Sir Walter, 1552–1618, English courtier, writer and
    adventurer   100, 197
Richard of Chichester, 1197–1253, Bishop of Chichester   174
Rinkart, Martin, 1586–1649, German minister and poet   165
Rolle, Richard, 1290–1349, Yorkshire hermit and spiritual writer
    72, 110
Rossetti, Christina, 1830–94, British poet   95, 113, 116, 142, 149,
    155, 213, 215, 240
Rutherford, Samuel, 1600–61, Scottish Presbyterian minister   51,
    204

Sarum Missal, 1085, a liturgy used widely in pre-Reformation
    England   100
Scott, Sir Walter, 1771–1832, Scottish historical novelist   204
Serenity Prayer, The, attributed to Reinhold Niebuhr, 1892–1971,
    theologian   140
Shaftesbury, Lord Anthony Ashley Cooper, 1801–85, social
    reformer   180, 244

Sidney, Philip, 1554–86, English poet and soldier   204

Simeon, Charles, 1759–1836, Vicar of Holy Trinity Church in Cambridge   205

Smart, Christopher, 1722–71, English poet   139

Spenser, Edmund, ?1552–99, English poet   239

Stephen, martyrdom recorded in the Acts of the Apostles   205

Stevenson, Robert Louis, 1850–94, Scottish travel writer and novelist   131, 212

Tait, Campbell, 1811–82, Archbishop of Canterbury   187

Tate, Nahum, 1652–1715, Poet Laureate   134, 164

Taylor, James Hudson, 1832–1905, pioneer missionary to China   205

Taylor, Jeremy, 1613–67, Anglican Bishop of Down and Connor   11, 64, 96

Te Deum Laudamus, author unknown   54

Temple, William, 1881–1944, Archbishop of Canterbury   140, 149

Tennyson, Lord Alfred, 1809–92, Poet Laureate   65

✳ Teresa of Avila, 1515–82, Spanish Carmelite mystic   6, 167, 205

Teresa, Mother, of Calcutta, 1910–98, founder of the Order of the Missionaries of Charity   176

Thackeray, William Makepeace, 1811–63, English writer   11

Thérèse of Lisieux, 1873–97, French nun   7

Toplady, Augustus Montague, 1740–78, hymn writer   205, 221

Traherne, Thomas, 1637–74, Anglican mystical poet   148

Treasury of Devotion, The, 1869   104, 114, 131, 132, 179, 226, 241

Tusser, Thomas, 1524–80   154

Tyndale, William, c. 1492–1536, English reformer and Bible translator   185

Upham, Thomas Cogswell, 1799–1872   24

Ussher, James, 1581–1656, Archbishop of Armagh and biblical scholar   67

Walton, Izaak, 1593–1683, English writer   243

Watts, Isaac, 1674–1748, nonconformist pastor and hymn writer   162, 225

Wesley, Charles, 1707–88, English clergyman and great hymn
writer 82, 115, 119, 170, 187, 198, 205, 238, 244
Wesley, John, 1703–91, founder of Methodism 9, 11, 78, 101,
121, 177, 205
Westcott, Brooke Foss, Bishop of Durham, leading Bible scholar
71, 102, 105, 117, 167
Whitefield, George, 1740–70, Methodist evangelist 205
Whittier, John Greenleaf, 1807–92, Quaker poet 79
Wilkinson, Kate B., 1859–1928, hymn writer 53
Wilson, Thomas, 1663–1755, Bishop of Sodor and Man 182
Winkworth, Catherine, pioneer of women's education and
hymn writer 165, 193
Wither, George, 1588–1667, English poet and Puritan
pamphleteer 126
Wordsworth, Christopher, 1807–85, Bishop of Lincoln, nephew
of William Wordsworth 52

Xavier, Francis, 1506–52, Jesuit teacher and pioneer missionary
to India and Japan 172

INDEX OF FIRST LINES

A short prayer finds its way to heaven   59

A wise lover values not so much the gift of the lover, as the love of the giver   7

Abide with me; fast falls the eventide   188

Abide with us, O Lord, for it is toward evening   132

After the *bread* and *wine* are deputed by holy prayer to God   106

All people that on earth do dwell   55

All shall be well, and all shall be well, and all manner of things shall be well   181

All that you do for love is love   8

Almighty and everlasting God, who for the well-being of our earthly life   102

Almighty and merciful God, into whose gracious presence we ascend   241

Almighty, eternal God, Father of our Lord Jesus Christ   134

Almighty, everlasting God, I draw near to the sacrament of your only-begotten Son   108

Almighty Father, grant that our universities and colleges   155

Almighty God, eternal Father of our Lord Jesus Christ   242

Almighty God, Father of our Lord Jesus Christ, establish and confirm us in your truth   88

Almighty God, in whom we live and move and have our being   54

Almighty God, in whose hands are all the powers of men   102

Almighty God, teach us by your holy Spirit   138

Almighty God, the Father of our Lord Jesus Christ, who has given you new birth   84
Almighty God, who has given your only Son to die for us   105
Almighty God, who hast given us grace at this time with one accord to make our common supplications   64
Almighty God, who hast given us thy only-begotten Son to take our nature upon him   213
Almighty God, who knows our necessities before we ask   168
Almighty God, who through the death of your Son has destroyed sin and death   240
Amazing grace! how sweet the sound   80
And by his stripes we are healed   3
And help us, this day and every day   142
And I know He loveth me!   3
And they shall be my people   3
And they stoned Stephen as he was calling on God and saying   205
And to him my soul shall live   3
And we shall be his people   3
Angels, from the realms of glory   212
Arise! Shine! Thy light has come!   3
As pants the hart for cooling streams   134
Awake, my soul, and with the sun   129
Awake, O my soul, awake!   3
Away with these filthy garments   203

Batter my heart, three-person'd God, for you   82
Be gracious to me, O God   3
Be of good comfort, brother, for we shall have a merry supper with the Lord this night   200
Be of good comfort, Master Ridley, and play the man   203
Be pleased, O God, to deliver me   8
Be thou a light to my eyes, music to my ears   97
Be thou my vision, O Lord of my heart   132
Beautiful   200
Beauty is God's handwriting   149
Because of me you bear fruit   3

Behold, Lord, an empty vessel that needs to be filled   117
Beside the waters of peace   3
Bless the Lord, O my soul, and all that is within me, bless his
    holy name   8, 21
Blessed are you, O Lord, the God of our ancestor Israel   54
Blessed be the God and Father of our Lord Jesus Christ, the
    Father of mercies   185
Blessed Jesus, you are always near in times of stress   159
Blessed Lord, who was tempted in all things just as we are   117
Breathe in me, O Holy Spirit   121
Breathe on me, Breath of God   118
Bring us, O Lord God, at our last awakening into the house and
    gate of heaven   197
But God is rich in mercy   3

Catherine of Siena made a cell in her heart   61
Change the world, O Lord, beginning with me   8
Clothe me, clothe me with yourself, eternal truth   51
Come, Almighty to deliver   244
Come, Holy Ghost, our souls inspire   242
Come, Holy Spirit, and daily increase in these your servants   88
Come, Lord Jesus   8
Come, Lord, work on us   51
Come, my Way, my Truth, my Life   52
Come, thou Father of the poor   3
Comfort ye, comfort ye my people, saith your God   172
Complete Thy work, O Lord, and as Thou hast loved me from
    the beginning   8
Create a clean heart in me   3

Dear Jesus, help me to spread your fragrance everywhere
    I go   178
Dear Lord and Father of mankind   79
Dearest Lord, teach me to be generous   178
Death be not proud, though some have callèd thee   192
Deliver me, Lord God, from a slothful mind, from all
    lukewarmness   101

'Do not pray for healing' 203
Drop, drop, slow tears 77

Earth is receding 204
Eternal God, the light of the minds that know Thee 173
Eternal God, the refuge of all your children 175
Eternal goodness, You want me to gaze into You 6
Eternal Light, shine into our hearts 99
Even such is time, that takes in trust 197

Father, forgive them, for they know not what they do 201
Father, into thy hands I commend my spirit 201
Father, make us more like Jesus 197
Father of Heaven, and Him, by whom 243
Fill me with joy and gladness 3
Fill Thou my life, O Lord my God 165
Finish, then, Thy new creation 198
For God is at work in me 4
For the beauty of the earth 150
For there is no other name 4
Forgive me, Lord, for thy dear Son 187
Forgive them all, O Lord 78
Forth in your name, O Lord I go 170
From death to life 195

Give me grace, Lord, to be strong, prudent, just and wise in all
    things 156
Give me my scallop-shell of quiet 100
Give us, O Lord, a steadfast heart, which no unworthy affection
    may drag downwards 103
Give us, O Lord, purity of lips 142
Give us the will, O God 154
Give us true humility, a meek and a quiet spirit 97
Glory be to God for dappled things 147
Glory be to God in the highest, Help us not to stray from you,
    for you are the Way 83

Glory be to God in the highest, Lord of heaven and earth   82
Glory be to Thee, O Lord, who makest Thine own Body and
   Blood to become our spiritual food   109
Glory to God for all things   9
Glory to the Lamb of God   4
Glory to thee, my God, this night   131
Go and bear fruit that will last   4
God Almighty bless us with his Holy Spirit this day   137
God be in my head   141
God be merciful to me, a sinner   9
God bless all those that I love   134
God gave me a message to deliver and a horse to ride   204
God, give us the serenity to accept what cannot be changed
   140
God guide me with your wisdom   152
God, I thank you for this day   45
God is as truly our Mother as he is our Father   122
God is worthy of our praise   4
God knows all things. He knows what we wish even before we
   ask for it   72
God so loved the world   203
God the Father bless me, Christ guard me, the Holy Spirit
   enlighten me, all the days of my life!   244
God the Father bless me; Jesus Christ defend and keep me   131
God that madest earth and heaven   196
God's child in Christ adopted, – Christ my all   154
Good Jesus, strength of the weary   135
Good Lord, you have refreshed our souls with the streams of
   knowledge   156
Grace and glory he bestows   4
Grace be with you   9
Gracious Father, I humbly beseech Thee for Thy Holy Catholic
   Church   125
Grant, Lord God, that in the middle of all the discouragements
   182
Grant, Lord God, that we may cleave to Thee without parting
   173

Grant, O Lord, that we may live in Thy fear   188
Grant, O Lord, to all students   155
Grant to us your servants: to our God – a heart of flame   179
Grant to your servants, O God, to be set on fire with
    your love   95
Grant us, Lord, to know in weakness the strength of your
    incarnation   153
Grant us, we beseech thee, O Lord, grace to follow thee
    withersoever thou goest   142
Grant, we beseech thee, almighty and merciful God, that the
    Holy Ghost may come upon us   241
Grant, we pray, Lord our God, that in whatever dangers we are
    placed   169
Grow old along with me!   190
Guide us, teach us, and strengthen us, O Lord   141

Happy are those whose transgression is forgiven, whose sin is
    covered   13
Have mercy on me, O God   4
Have mercy on me, O God, according to your steadfast love
    75
He is our clothing   6
He is our God, if we despair in ourselves and trust in him   185
He let us share in His spirit   4
He who has a heart full of love always has something
    to give   7
Hear while I tell about the best of dreams   223
Heavenly Father, I most heartily thank thee   136
Help me now, O God, to do all things in your sight, who sees
    in secret   114
Help me, O God, like Jesus to be growing all the time   9, 114
Here am I, the servant of the Lord   9
Here is the heaven of heaven!   86
Here die I, Richard Grenville   202
Here, O my Lord, I see thee face to face   108
Him alone you shall adore   4
His eye is on the sparrow   4

His love is everlasting   4

His praise endures forever   4

Holy, holy, holy Lord   4

'Holy, holy, holy, the Lord God the Almighty   60

Holy is the Lamb of God   4

Holy Spirit, as the wind is Thy symbol, so forward our
    goings   116

How good is the God we adore   151

How good is the Lord to all   4

How lovely is your dwelling place, O Lord of hosts!   12

How right it is to love you   4

How sweet the name of Jesus sounds   164

I am in Love, and out of it I will not go   6

I am not come hither to deny my Lord and Master   199

I am not tired of my work, neither am I tired of the world   202

I am ready to die for my Lord   199

I am so weak that I can hardly write   205

I am tired in the Lord's work   205

I ask not to see; I ask not to know; I ask only to be used   9

I asked God for strength, that I might achieve   111

I asked the Lord, that I might grow   117

I beg you, dearest brethren, love one another   200

I bind to myself the name   81

I bind unto myself today   160

I do not regret that I have given myself to love   7

I do not think that in the last forty years   244

I give my dying testimony to the truth of Christianity   203

I got me flowers to strew thy way   236

I have been given mercy   4

I have called you by your name   4

I have grasped you by the hand   4

I have heard a grave divine say   243

I have no wit, no words, no tears   240

I have pain   199

I lift up my eyes to the hills – from where will my help
    come?   16

I love the Lord, because he has heard my voice and my
    supplications   14
I offer up unto you my prayers and intercessions   78
I rise today with the power of God to guide me   113
I shall be satisfied with thy likeness   205
I sought Him whom my heart loves   4
I thirst   201
I urge upon you communion with Christ, a growing
    communion   51
I was a stricken deer, that left the herd   158
I will never be ashamed to render an account of my profession
    and of that hope that is in me   73
I will never forget you   4
I wish to be alone, with my God   205
I'm so thankful for active obedience of Christ   203
If ask'd, what of Jesus I think?   104
If he should slay me ten thousand times   204
If [the Bible] is, as we devoutly believe, the very source and
    measure of our religious faith   71
If you get simple beauty and naught else   147
In a religious sense, meditation is such an application of the
    mind to the consideration of any divine subject   72
In age and feebleness extreme   187
In his love he clothes us   185
In his quiver he hid me   4
In the bleak mid-winter   215
In the hour of my distress   86
In these our days so perilous   174
In you I hope all day long   4
In you I place all my trust   4
In your love remember me   4
Incline us, O God, to think humbly on ourselves   96
Into your hands, O Lord, I commend my spirit   132
Is this a Fast, to keep   217
It is a thing most wonderful   222
It is finished   201
It is good to mistrust ourselves   66

It will be of great importance if you can leave the care of your
  affairs   58
Jesu, grant me this, I pray   191, 221
Jesu, lover of my soul, let me to Thy bosom fly   115
Jesus, as a mother you gather your people to you   182
Jesus Christ is risen today, Alleluya!   239
Jesus is the Lamb of God   5
Jesus, strengthen my desire to work and speak and think
  for you   9
Jesus taught men to see the operation of God in the regular and
  the normal   149
Jesus, the very thought of thee   138
Joy cometh in the morning   5
Just as I am, without one plea   85

Keep us, Lord, so awake in the duties of our callings   138
Keep us steadfast in your love   5
Keep your eyes fixed on Jesus   5
King of glory, King of peace   124

Lead, Kindly Light, amid the encircling gloom   194
Let all mortal flesh keep silent, and with fear and trembling
  stand   122
Let go and let God   5
Let man's Soul be a Sphere   219
Let my soul spend itself in Your praise, rejoicing for love   7
Let not your heart be troubled   192
Let nothing cause thy heart to fail   202
Let nothing disturb you   167
Let our chief goal, O God, be your glory, and to enjoy you for
  ever   9
Let silence be your wisdom   5
Let the eternal God be the portion of my soul   98
Let the healing waters flow   5
Let the root of love be within   7
Let the words of my mouth and the meditation of my heart be
  acceptable to you   9

Let this day, O Lord, add some knowledge or good deed to
    yesterday   10
Let us love, for love will give us everything   8
Live in Christ, live in Christ, and the flesh need not
    fear death   203
Lord, almighty God, Father of your beloved and blessed Son
    Jesus Christ, through whom we have come   199
Lord, almighty God, Father of your beloved and blessed Son
    Jesus Christ   199
Lord, bless all means that are used for my recovery   157
Lord, give me what you are requiring of me   10
Lord, give us faith that right makes might   10
Lord, give us weak eyes for things which are of no account
    153
Lord God, you have sent out your light   133
Lord, help me   10
Lord, help us to be masters of ourselves, that we may be servants
    of others   176
Lord, however Thou dispose of me, continue and go on to do
    good for them   201
Lord, I am blind and helpless   153
Lord, I am indeed unworthy that you should come under
    my roof   106
Lord, I am yours   92
Lord, I believe; help thou mine unbelief   9
Lord, I believe in you – increase my faith   93
Lord Jesus Christ, Son of God, have mercy on me, a sinner   10
Lord Jesus Christ, true Man and God   193
Lord Jesus Christ, who for the redemption of the world
    ascended the wood of the cross   227
Lord Jesus, I give you my hands to do your work   102
Lord, let your glory be my goal, your word my rule, and then
    your will be done   10
Lord, make me according to your heart   10
Lord, make me an instrument of your peace   175
Lord, make me see your glory in every place   10
Lord, our God, we are in the shadow of your wings   190

Lord, purge our eyes to see   149
Lord, remember me when thou comest into thy kingdom   9
Lord, save me   10
Lord, teach me the art of patience   136
Lord, teach us to number our days, that we may apply our
    hearts to wisdom   140
Lord, thank you that in your love you have taken from me all
    earthly riches   191
Lord, who createdst man in wealth and store   235
Lord, you commanded peace   135
Love bade me welcome: yet my soul drew back   81
Love came down at Christmas   213
Love divine, all loves excelling   82
Love does not consist in shedding tears   6
Love is a mighty power, a great and complete good   7
Love is kind and suffers long   52
Love my memory   204
Love's redeeming work is done   238

Make me, O my God, humble without pretence   133
Make me remember, O God, that every day is Thy gift   138
Mark you the floor? That square and speckled stone   98
May Christ support us all the day long   132
May God be with you and bless you   157
May our dear Lord Jesus Christ show you his hands and
    his side   223
May our Lord Jesus Christ bless you   216
May the grace of Christ our Saviour   141
May the Lord keep our going out and our coming in   140
May the love of the Lord Jesus draw us to Himself   140
May the mind of Christ my Saviour   53
Make us worthy, Lord   176
Meditation alone is the remedy of security and worldliness   72
More things are wrought by prayer than this world
    dreams of   65
Most glorious Lord of Life, that on this day   239
Most high, most great and good Lord, to you belong praises   150

Most loving Lord, give me a childlike love of thee   163
My cup is overflowing   5
My dearest Lord, be Thou a bright flame before me   15
My God and My All!   10
My God, I give you this day   126
My God, I pray that I may so know you and love you   143
My God, make haste to help me!   5
My God, My God, why hast thou forsaken me?   201
My God, my God, why have you forsaken me?   218
My grace is enough for you   5
My Heavenly Father knows   5
My Jesus, my King, my Life, my All   155
My life is spent with sorrow   5
My Lord and my God   10
My Lord and my God, take me from all that keeps me from
    you   104
My Lord, I have nothing to do in this world but to seek and
    serve you   174
My peace is my gift to you   5
My song is love unknown   183
My soul magnifies the Lord   5
My spirit is dry within me because it forgets to feed on you
    117
My spirit longs for Thee   52
My stock lies dead, and no increase   111
My words and thoughts do both express this notion   206

New every morning is the love   128
Now comes the mystery   199
Now thank we all our God   165

O all ye, who pass by, whose eyes and mind   229
O almighty God, who has built your church on the foundations
    of the apostles and prophets   125
O Christ, give us patience and faith and hope as we kneel at
    the foot of thy Cross   223
O come, let us adore Him   5

O eternal God and merciful Father, look down upon me in mercy 196

O Father of heaven, O Son of God, Redeemer of the world 194

O for a closer walk with God 103

O God and Lord of the Powers, and Maker of all creation 114

O God, by thy mercy strengthen us who lie exposed to the rough storms of troubles and temptations 113

O God, give me strength 11

O God, give us work 171

O God, help us not to despise or oppose what we do not understand 11

O God, keep me from being difficult to live with 11

O God, make us children of quietness and heirs of peace 126

O God of all power, you called from death the great pastor of the sheep 169

O God of all the nations of the earth 172

O God of peace, good beyond all that is good 125

O God, our Help in ages past 162

O God, our loving Father, help us rightly to remember the birth of Jesus 212

O God, the Father of the forsaken 180

O God, to me who am left to mourn his departure 186

O God who has ordained that whatever is to be desired should be sought by labour 190

O God, who has warned us that you will require much from those to whom much is given 176

O God, who makes us glad with the yearly remembrance of the birth of your only Son Jesus Christ 215

O God, who resists the proud, and gives grace to the humble 96

O God, you have dealt very mysteriously with us 187

O God, you know my folly 11

O good Shepherd, seek me, and bring me home to your fold again 91

O happy day, that fixed my choice 89

O Heart of Love, I believe in Your goodness 8

O holy Child of Bethlehem   211
O holy simplicity!   202
O innocent Jesus, who with wonderful submission wast for our
sakes condemned to die   226
O Jesus, fill me with your love now   174
O Jesus, I have promised   88
O Joy that seekest me through pain   186
O Lord and Master of my life   112
O Lord, baptize our hearts into a sense of the needs and
conditions of all   176
O Lord, calm the waves of this heart, calm its tempest!   159
O Lord, deprive me not of your heavenly blessings   127
O Lord, enlighten my heart   138
O Lord, evening is at hand   189
O Lord, give our blessing, we pray, to our daily work   171
O Lord, give us, we beseech Thee, in the name of Jesus Christ
Thy Son our Lord, that love which can never cease   63
O Lord God, in whom we live and move and have our
being   167
O Lord God of our salvation, to whom no sickness is
incurable   158
O Lord God of time and eternity   155
O Lord God, *our Father in heaven*   137
O Lord God, when Thou givest to Thy servants to endeavour
any great matter   99
O Lord, I do not pray for tasks equal to my strength   170
O Lord Jesus Christ, who on the first day of the week rose
again   209
O Lord Jesus Christ, who though you were rich became
poor   179
O Lord, let us not live to be useless, for Christ's sake   11
O Lord, look mercifully on us, and grant that we may always
choose the way of peace   100
O Lord, never allow us to think we can stand by ourselves and
not need you   11
O Lord of all worlds   186

O Lord our God, grant us, we beseech thee, patience in
troubles   116

O Lord our God, teach us to ask aright for the right
blessings   168

O Lord, remember not only the men and women of good
will   177

O Lord seek us, O Lord find us   113

O Lord, take full possession of my heart   121

O Lord, the Scripture says, 'There is a time for silence and a
time for speech.'   120

O Lord, thou knowest how busy I must be this day   170

O Lord, who has brought us through the darkness of night
136

O love eternal, my soul needs and chooses you eternally   120

O Love, O God, you created me, in your love recreate me   91

O Love that wilt not let me go   53

O loving Christ, draw me, a weakling   198

O my Saviour, and my God, let it come   139

O my strength, for you I watch   5

O send out your light and your truth   11

O thou who camest from above   119

O, that we might know the Lord!   5

Of the love of God, there are various kinds   24

Only in God be at rest   5

Open my eyes that I may see   97

Oppressed with sin and woe   76

Our baptism is to signify our seeking and obtaining a new
birth   83

Our Father in heaven   22

Our Father which in Heaven art   126

Our Father, you called us and saved us in order to make us like
your Son   120

Our Saviour Christ is both the first beginner of our spiritual
life   105

Praise, my soul, the King of heaven   123

Praise to the Holiest in the height   56

Pray God, keep us simple 11
Prayer is the ascent of the mind to God 64
Prayer is the soul's sincere desire 59
Prayer, the Church's banquet, Angels' age 63
Protect me, dear Lord; My boat is so small 161
Put off thy robe of purple, then go on 228

Rain, do not hurt my flowers, but quickly spread 181
Remember, Christian soul 139
Remember that nothing is small in the eyes of God 7
Remember your mercies, Lord 5
Renewal does not happen in one moment of conversion 84
Ride on! ride on in majesty! 218
Rock of ages, cleft for me 221

Save me, O God, for the waters have come up to my neck 18
See in what peace a Christian can die 199
See now, I commend my soul to God for whom I am an
    ambassador 204
Seek the things that are above 5
Send out your light and your truth 92
Set a watch, O Lord, before my mouth, and keep the door of
    my lips 104
Set free, O Lord, the souls of your servants from all restlessness
    and anxiety 167
Shine from the cross to me, then all is peace 185
Shout joyfully to God, all the earth 209
Sir Walter Scott expressed the wish 204
So we must either love or die, because he who does not love
    remains a dead person 7
Solitariness of place is the most appropriate place for
    meditation 62
Sometimes a light surprises 181
Speak, for your servant is listening 11
Speak, Lord, for Thy servant heareth 95
Strengthen me, O God, by the grace of your Holy Spirit 166
Strengthen us, O God, to relieve the oppressed 178

Take for your motto: Love has conquered me   6

Take from us, O God, all tediousness of spirit, all impatience
    and unquietness   96

Take, Lord, and receive all my liberty   96

Take my life, and let it be   91

Take time to think: it is the source of power   44

Taste and see that the Lord is good   5

Teach me, my God and King   170

Teach me to pray. Pray yourself in me   11

Teach us to pray often, that we may pray oftener   11

Thanks be to Thee, Lord Jesus Christ   174

The best of all is, God is with us   205

The best prayers have more often groans than words   63

The closer and more present God is to a soul, the purer is his
    love   110

The Father and I are one   5

The first rule of right prayer is to have our heart and mind
    framed   65

The fog is rising   201

The God of love my shepherd is   163

The grace of the Lord Jesus be with all the saints   12

The hand of the Lord feeds me   5

The hatred which divides nation from nation   94

The hour I have long wished for is now come   205

The Lord is my light and my salvation   161

The Lord is my rock, my fortress, and my deliverer   166

The Lord keeps the little ones   5

The Lord make you holy and bless you   156

The love of Christ compels us   5

The Sacred Three   157

The shepherds sing; and shall I be silent?   214

The sky is clear; there is no cloud   205

The things, good Lord, that we pray for, give us the grace to
    labour for   12

The victory of justice   6

There can be nothing either more necessary or profitable, than
    the knowledge of Holy Scripture   66

Think upon all His wonders   6
This Holy Scripture, thus written in Hebrew and Greek   66
'Though I have endeavoured to avoid sin'   200
Though the fig tree does not blossom   180
Through all the changing scenes of life   164
Thy way, not mine, O Lord   152
To begin ... with traditions   67
To know that Love alone was the beginning of nature and
     creature   161
To love God is something greater than to know him   7
To Mercy, Pity, Peace, and Love   182
To pray in the Spirit is the inward principle of prayer   63
To thee, O God, we turn for peace   168
To you, O Lord, I lift up my soul   16
Today shalt thou be with me in paradise   201
Tomorrow shall be my dancing day   236
'Twas God the word that spake it   105

Unless the Lord builds the house   156
Use me, my Saviour, for whatever purpose and in what way you
     require   177

Wait for the Lord   12
We beg you, Lord, to help and defend us   179
We beseech you, O Lord, to purify our consciences by your
     daily visitation   211
We bring before you, O Lord   180
We feed on what we read, but we digest only what we meditate
     of   71
We give thanks to you, almighty God, that you have refreshed
     us with this salutary gift   108
We give thanks to you, heavenly Father, through Jesus Christ
     your dear Son   133
We have been given mercy   6
We offer you immortal praise and thanks   109
We plough the fields and scatter   210

We praise thee, O God, we acknowledge thee to be the
   Lord   54
We resign into your hands our sleeping bodies   131
We should love God because He is God   7
Welcome to the Table   107
What a man is on his knees before God   64
What can be more excellent than prayer   65
When, as a child, I laughed and wept   193
When I am gone, speak less of Dr Carey and more of Dr
   Carey's Saviour   200
When I consider how my light is spent   158
When I survey the wondrous Cross   225
While women weep, as they do now, I'll fight   200
Who is this king of glory?   6
Who would true valour see   99
Why are you cast down, O my soul   159
Will you not revive us again   12
Will you see the infancy of this sublime and celestial
   greatness?   148
Wilt Thou forgive that sin where I begun   76
With God I shall do bravely   6
Woman, behold thy Son   201
Worth more than many sparrows   6
Worthy is the Lamb of God   6
Write your blessed name, O Lord, upon my heart   169

You are holy, Lord, the only God   57
You are my strength and my song   6
You are never tired, O Lord, of doing us good   177
You are now going to burn a goose   202
You are worthy, our Lord and God   23
You have been given mercy   6
You have been used to take notice of the sayings of dying
   men   202
You have made us for yourself and our hearts are restless until
   in you they find their rest   12

You tell me nothing new: you are not the only one that is
    troubled with wandering thoughts   61
You will tell the others I am going home a little sooner than I
    thought   204